THE LITTLE BOOK for the soul

an ancient healing process

Sandra L. Butler

Library of Congress cataloging in Publication data:

Butler, Sandra L.
The Little Book for the Soul
ISBN-9780967729671

2020 Final Edition
ISBN-9780578815480

Published by
Gilead Publishing Company

Cover Design by Creative Image Design, Bozeman, Montana

With sincere gratitude for the Spirit of truth.

Try first thyself, and after call in God;
For to the worker God himself lends aid.
Hippolytus

Table of Contents

Foreword

THE LITTLE BOOK for the soul is a supplement to the author's first book— *The Bible Decoded: breaking the ancient code.* It is the detailed account of the healing process encoded in *The Holy Bible*— an ancient instruction that comes to us aptly through the book of *Genesis,* meaning *creation,* describing the process educed through the application of this spiritual knowledge. Through six metaphorical days of spiritual works we become a new creation, experiencing the best possible life in the physical realm and the highest degree of life in the spiritual realm. This state was reached by one who combined the ancient practices of the east with the ancient instruction found in the Sacred Text of the west, becoming the greatest ascended master of all— *Jesus the Christ.*

An in-depth understanding of this phenomenal healing process required word knowledge, symbolic understanding, and firsthand experience. The process is brilliantly encoded in the creation story in the beginning of Genesis and in the last words of Jacob to his twelve sons in the end of Genesis. Through its completion, we are healed mentally and emotionally, the positive energy from this transformation process moving out to heal the body of its many infirmities, allowing us the freedom to enjoy the pleasures of life without pain, fear, or the burden of addiction. This is true salvation, the freeing of the soul.

Introduction

THE LITTLE BOOK for the soul depicts our journey through life, our path determined by our mind, in which exist 12 gates that lead into our heart, as the 12 gates in the wall of Jerusalem lead into the temple. God is the *Father,* the author of life. But we are the book, inscribing words upon its pages through life experiences. Writing a true word upon the tablets of our heart sowed the good seed, ascribing to the *Son* of God. Writing a false word sowed the evil seed, attributed to the son of perdition. The power that sows the good seed, is *Holy Spirit—* a positive and constructive energy. But the power that sows the evil seed is negative and destructive. We have all eaten of the tree of the knowledge of good and evil, sowing both seeds. And in the process of time, the evil choked out the good, resulting in a life that we may no longer take much joy in.

The 12 sons of Jacob are the12 tribes of Israel, which are neither lost nor extinct, but existing within. By judging the negative aspects of these sons or tribes, we take possession of the positive, claiming our Father's spiritual inheritance by taking possession of a spiritual promised land— a life of joy and contentment. Through the creation of a new spiritual heaven and a new earth we become a new creation, rewriting the book of our life, receiving a new name and the salvation of our soul through that anointing called *christ.*

The journey of the children of Israel gives us insight into our journey through life. We are the spiritual children of Israel, and being children are taught the spiritual things of God through repetition, brilliantly accomplished through the intriguing, and sometimes perplexing stories of the Bible.

Chapter One
In the Beginning

In the beginning God created the heaven and the earth. And the earth was without form, and void; and darkness was upon the face of the deep. And the Spirit of God moved upon the face of the waters. And God said, Let there be light: and there was light. And God saw the light, that it was good: and God divided the light from the darkness.

Genesis 1:1-4

In the beginning, before our earthly bodies took form, we were void, containing no matter. We were formed in darkness, in a womb of water upon which spirit or energy would move, bringing on the contractions that through the process of time delivered us into the light. We entered this world in accordance with God's Law— moved by spirit and brought into light. This law extends beyond the physical and into the spiritual, which remains in effect throughout our life. As long as we were moved by our holy spirit we remained in the light, making the right choices, which had positive and constructive consequences. But when we began to be influenced by an unholy spirit we brought ourselves into darkness, becoming confused, making wrong choices, which had negative and destructive consequences. To revert to our former condition, returning to that state of existence we once knew as little children, we must create and form a new heaven and earth by following God's creation process.

In the midst of the garden stood the tree of life and the tree of the knowledge of good and evil. We are that tree, and throughout our life, through human experience, we came to know both good and evil. The evil caused a separation from our elevated state of existence, driving us out of our place of protection, bringing pain and troubles into our life. The tree, whose leaves take in the generous waters from above, have roots that reach out into darkness, drawing in the waters from below— an analogy to the *firmament* in God's creation. Our mind is the firmament, expanding through thought, standing between the waters above the firmament (positive and constructive thoughts) and the waters below the firmament (negative and destructive thoughts). This firmament called *heaven* is a spiritual kingdom— the *kingdom of heaven,* symbolizing the *realm of the mind,* which being influenced by the things we saw, heard, felt, and experienced has taken in thoughts that were right and thoughts that were in error; taking in the knowledge of good and evil.

The kingdom of heaven is like unto a net, that was cast into the sea, and gathered every kind: Which, when full, they drew to shore, and sat down, and gathered the good into vessels, but cast the bad away.
Matthew 13:47,48

The spirit that moves upon or influences the waters or thoughts of our mind is either positive or negative. The positive spirit or energy is our holy spirit, which brings light; awareness of the negative and destructive thoughts hidden in the depths of our mind; those lower waters called the *sea.* It is going to take this holy spirit, a degree of pain, and hard labor to deliver the truth that makes the creation of our new mind and heart possible, bringing us back into a joyous life. When does this internal spiritual creation process begin to take place? When we look at our life and see that it is not all that we would like it to be. What we have imagined our life to be is not what it is. It is in this moment of realization or crisis

2

that our heart cries out, activating our holy spirit, caretaker of the heart. The purpose of this divine energy is not only to sustain the life of our physical body, but to maintain the life of our ethereal or spiritual body.

Spirit, in conjunction with the *Word,* moves us out of oppression, depression, affliction, and addiction; moving us out of spiritual bondage, as *Moses,* in conjunction with *Aaron,* moved the children of Israel out of physical bondage when their cry came up before God. It was through these two witnesses that the children of Israel were moved up out of Egypt, through the wilderness, and into a new land, being transplanted; uprooted from bondage and sowed into freedom; a transition that can only take place by traversing that spiritual wilderness called the mind, which is renewed through the transformation of the heart, changing the negative and destructive way we think, feel, and act forever! This is salvation of the soul!

And God said, Let there be a firmament in the midst of these waters, and let it divide the waters from the waters. Genesis 1:6

The function of the mind or *firmament* called *heaven* is to divide the upper and lower waters; the positive and constructive thoughts from the negative and destructive thoughts. If the mind had done this in the beginning, our life would be perfect, the result of making all the right decisions from a right spirit and word. But we were children, often influenced by a wrong spirit and word. And being naive children, we divided them for the evil by accepting lies as truth, and then pushing these negative and destructive thoughts down into the darkness of repression, separating them from the light of truth, and from the conscious mind.

And God called the firmament Heaven... And God said, Let the waters under the heaven be gathered together into one place, and let the dry land appear: and it was so. Genesis 1:8,9

3

God instructs us to gather *the waters under the heaven* together, bringing *the thoughts or memories hidden in the depths of our mind,* which contain negative and destructive energy, into one place; into our awareness. Continuing to repress them will not make them go away. And controlling our thoughts or programming our mind to concentrate only on the good thoughts; *"the waters above the firmament,"* is not in accordance with the Word of God when it comes to the creation process. It is only by bringing our attention to these lower waters that we have the ability to see *dry land.*

And God called the dry land Earth; and the gathering together of the waters called he Seas: and God saw that it was good. Genesis 1:10

The *Earth* symbolizes the *Heart.* The *Seas* or lower waters symbolize our *well-hidden thoughts or memories.* When we allow these waters to be gathered together into one place through the power of our holy spirt, which Moses illustrated when he stretched his hand out over the Sea, we begin to see salvation, which for the Israelites came in the form of dry land, earth. When we allow our holy spirit to move these repressed memories into our awareness, we see what lies beneath them in that spiritual earth called the heart as we begin to feel the painful emotions we have suppressed for all these years. It is this painful emotional energy that empowers our word of error; the evil seeds of false beliefs, which cause our sorrow and suffering, fueling our bondages or addictions.

Prerequisite for the Process

When the children of Israel were about to escape the bondage of Egypt, the heart of Pharaoh, ruler of that land, was hardened. We are our own Pharaoh, ruler of Egypt, symbolizing our world or realm of existence, which we created and formed. We can remain in our current state through stubbornness, or be delivered from it through humility. The process is activated by desire. And it will be our continued desire and commitment to change that will ensure its success and completion. When we desire positive change in our life, that desire releases a compassionate energy that will bring about situations in our life that will motivate us, illustrated by the plagues in Egypt, which got the Israelites moving. It is in these times of discomfort or difficulty that we often unwittingly cry out from our heart, causing the *holy spirit* to appear, activating the process that will deliver us from the burden of our word of error, as *Moses* appeared to deliver the children of Israel from the burden of bondage.

Exodus from Bondage

The children of Israel entered Egypt, where they remained free for *40 years, living under the rule of *Joseph* and the *kings* that knew Joseph, which is to be subject to *truth* and to *spirits* associated with truth. Upon the death of these kings, the children go into bondage for *390 years. We enter Egypt, symbolizing the World, at birth. As long as truth rules our heart we remain free. But when the lies of our mind are accepted by our heart as truth through the power of painful emotions we go into bondage; into spiritual addiction, which in the process of time moves out into the physical in the form of destructive behaviors. If we are taught from infancy that we have the power to control our external world, we would have blamed ourselves for every painful thing that occurred that was out of our control, telling ourselves that it was our fault, carrying the guilt; which compounded by the fear, gave power to the lies that we would speak repeatedly through our mind; a multitude of untruthful thoughts that just past the tender age of *4 began the process of becoming the false beliefs of our heart. These evil seeds, sown in the heart through the power of emotion by age six, would begin

5

to be demonstrated through destructive behaviors. Most of us will remain in bondage to these beliefs for about *39 years, after which time we begin our journey toward a new way of life, which for many will be ushered in by a mid-life crisis; a time when we seek to recapture our youth. But what we are really seeking to recapture is the freedom we felt as a little child through our holy spirit, which we began extinguishing early on through our many fears and misconceptions. The physical action we take during a mid-life crisis is really just a way in which we unwittingly attempt to combat the spiritual subversion of our holy spirit, which has been going on for years. * Egyptian time differs from our own by a factor of 10 to 1.

Preparing for the Process

All that is required for us to partake of this great salvation is a quiet mind, and a desire to learn about ourselves.

And Moses said unto all the people, Fear ye not, stand still, and see the salvation of the Lord… Exodus 14:13

The word *still* means *quiet self, be silent, keep (put to) silence.* Our world has become one of incessant noise and distractions. Our minds are constantly being bombarded. We sit in front of our screens where our minds are hit with a multitude of quick-cut images and sounds, while our children play in rooms piled high with toys, each one having the ability to capture their attention for about a minute. And we wonder why our children have a limited attention span? We call it a disorder, and give it a name, Attention Deficit Disorder or ADD. The solution is simple. We need to stop ADDing things to our life. We engage our children and ourselves in all kinds of activities, and all this input to mind and body keeps us separated from our heart, the seat of the emotions. The busier we can keep our mind and body, the less time we have to think about how we truly feel. And getting in touch with our emotions is the key that will open the door, releasing us from a spiritual prison of spiritual bondages.

The process combines the ancient mind-body discipline of the east with the ancient instruction found in the Sacred Text of the west, the perfect blending of spirit and word; the two witnesses that lead us out of bondage. The *seventh seal* or seventh chakra connects us to the divinity within, to our divine source; our holy spirit, a positive spiritual energy, a connection that requires *silence in heaven;* quiet in the mind.

Ancient instruction on meditation

And when he had opened the seventh seal, there was silence in heaven about the space of half an hour. Revelation 8:1

Set aside *half an hour* each day to be still in mind and body.

And the earth was without form, and void...

Set aside all incantations, mantras, or repetitious prayers, which are extraneous attachments to belief, creating the *void* that is needed for the new creation to begin.

and darkness was upon the face of the deep...

This means nothingness in the mind. No visualizations, no gazing at crystals, no making of sounds. Listen only to the primordial sound of your breath, the physical manifestation of the holy spirit.

And the Spirit of God moved upon the face of the waters.

When we quiet our mind we abase its power; the power of the mind giving way to the power or holy *spirit* of the heart, which void of all extraneous attachments, is free to move upon the waters, influencing the thoughts of our mind. It takes time to quiet the mind, to turn off the everyday thoughts, so be patient, *"But let patience have her perfect work"* (James 1:4), that perfect work being a complete transformation. When the ego-driven thoughts of the mind are restrained, the holy spirit of the heart is free to move the subconscious thoughts into the light; into the awareness of the conscious mind.

But lift thou up thy rod, and stretch out thine hand over the sea, and divide it... Exodus 14:16

The *rod* of discipline, applied to mind and body, gives power to the heart, evoking a more powerful mind-heart-body response, allowing for the complete salvation of the soul, the word soul defined as the vital principle in man credited to the faculty of thought, emotion, and action. Exercises that facilitate the process of opening the six energy centers of the body, while keeping the mind quiet are two eastern practices that will aid in the release work that is to follow.

The Process

The process has 12 steps or judgments, in which is 7 weeks of work. Seven, being the spiritual number, indicates an indeterminate period of time. The word *seven* means *seven times, to seven oneself,* correlating these seven spiritual weeks of work with the seven literal weeks that fall between Passover and Shabuoth or Feast of Weeks.

...Then went he down, and dipped himself seven times in Jordan... and his flesh came again like unto the flesh of a little child, and he was clean.
2 Kings 5:13,14

Our spiritual passover takes place when we make a decision to pass over from our old way of life into a new way of life. The seven weeks that follow represent the period of time in which we complete our six metaphorical days of spiritual works, resulting in the creation of a new heaven and earth; a new mind and heart, with a new way of thinking and believing, resulting in a new life. This new life has a numerical value of 1, which when added to 49, our seven spiritual weeks of spiritual works, brings us to 50; to our spiritual Jubilee, having been released from our spiritual bondage and spiritual debt through the completion of our spiritual works, which has led to the death of our old way of life. With our spiritual works and death complete, we enter our rest.

Jubilee, among the ancient Jews, extraordinary Sabbatical year (following every seventh ordinary Sabbatical year) celebrated every 50th year. In the year of Jubilee, the land was completely left to rest. All debts were remitted; land that had been alienated was restored to its original owners; and all Jews, who, through poverty, had obliged to hire themselves out as servants, were released from bondage. "Jubilee" Funk and Wagnall's New Encyclopedia.1986 ed.

The process can be divided into three phases, which are completed through three distinct powers. The first phase, which takes us through the first three sons of Jacob is accomplished through the power of the mind; knowledge. Through this phase we acknowledge the three spirits that rule our mind, heart, and body; our thoughts, feelings, and actions. The second phase, which takes us through the next seven sons of Jacob, is accomplished through the spontaneous power of the heart; understanding. It is here that we begin receiving *manna* from heaven as our mind begins to question things, the word *manna* meaning *what? how? why? when?* What happened? How, why, and when, did our heart become inhabited with the unholy spirits that made us subject to these false beliefs that keep us in bondage.

The third and final phase, which takes us through the last two sons of Jacob, is accomplished when we use the light of this understanding to complete the process that transforms or renews our mind and heart.

If you are accustomed to working a program, you may choose to do these weeks of work, consecutively. This disciplinary law, serving as a metaphorical school-master, will teach you to be mindful of the process, and familiar with its feeling, affecting a degree of change. But the liberating and everlasting effects of this process will be the result of the power of that spiritual womb called the heart, which the power of the mind cannot control or coerce into a fixed period of time. This process is the process of spiritual birth, which like physical birth, is natural, spontaneous, not forced. And while there is one process of birth, the experience, along with the degree of pain and length of labor, will be individual. This process or spiritual judgment, which the 12 sons of Jacob or 12 tribes of Israel represent, is the creation of our new spiritual heaven and earth, which is called *new Jerusalem*, symbolizing a *new peaceful state*.

And Jesus said unto them..., Verily I say unto you, That ye which have followed me, in the regeneration when the Son of man shall sit in the throne of his glory, ye also shall sit upon twelve thrones, judging the twelve tribes of Israel. Matthew 19:28

The word *regeneration* means *the act or process of re-forming, to create anew.*

And I saw a new heaven and a new earth: for the first heaven and the first earth were passed away; and there was no more sea. And I John saw the holy city, new Jerusalem, coming down from God out of heaven, prepared as a bride adorned for her husband... and there shall be no more death, neither sorrow, nor crying, neither shall there be any more pain: for the former things are passed away. And he that sat upon the throne said, Behold, I make all things new... Revelation 21:1-5

10

As you go through this process it is important to concentrate on the journey, not the destination. The mind, as a means of maintaining its control, will attempt to force things, rushing the process, sabotaging the spontaneous workings of your holy spirit, which is needed to complete your transformation. You may notice a surge of energy coming from within during and after this preparation work. In lifting up our holy spirit we increase its degree of energy, which is bound to bring on a power struggle as our unholy spirit of negative energy, which has been ruling over us for so long, rises up to maintain its control.

And the children struggled together within her... And the Lord said unto her, Two nations are in thy womb... Genesis 25:22,23

Identifying the energy, positive or negative, will be addressed in chapter four. But in the early stages of applying this process, the lies of our mind, empowered by the unholy spirit of fear, will try to convince us that this is nonsense. That it is unnecessary, or even counterproductive to engage in any discipline that will cause the negative and painful things from our past to come to the surface. It may tell us we are making a mountain out of a molehill that things are not really all that bad, and anything that needs to be resolved can be achieved by our old method of handling things. Don't buy it!

Chapter Two
The Sons of Jacob

And Jacob called unto his sons, and said, Gather yourselves together, that I may tell you that which shall befall you in the last days. Gather yourselves together, and hear, ye sons of Jacob: and hearken unto Israel your father.   *Genesis 49:1,2*

The word *befall* means *to encounter*, the words Jacob speaks to his sons revealing what we will encounter as we go through this process, one preserved for the end of days. As we advance through these twelve sons of Jacob we are to apply the message of each son to our life. Judging the negative aspects of these sons or tribes is taking the action needed to overcome them. Through this righteous judgment we overcome the negative aspects of the sons of Jacob, leaving us with the positive aspects of each *son of Jacob*, symbolizing the *fruit of the Spirit.*

But the fruit of the Spirit is love, joy, peace, longsuffering, gentleness, goodness, faith, meekness, temperance: against such there is no law.
Galatians 5:22,23

There is no law under God's spirit. Our limitations are the result of our own spirit, which gave power to our own word. This false word formed the invisible *flesh* that opposes God's *spirit*. It is this robe of internal sinful flesh that will limit us throughout our life.

For the flesh desires the contrary of the spirit, and the spirit the contrary of the flesh; for these are opposed to each other; so that you do not perform the things which you wish... Galatians 5:17,18

And the word was made flesh (John 1:14). The word of God was made flesh. But God's word, truth, which Jesus personified, carries no burden. It makes us free. It is our word of error that causes us to carry a heavy burden, which Jesus illustrated for us by carrying the cross. It is our word of error, sin that weighs heavily upon the truth, crucifying it daily.

And when this people, or the prophet, or a priest, shall ask thee, saying, What is the burden of the Lord? thou shalt say unto them, What burden?... And the burden of the Lord shall ye mention no more: for every man's word shall be his burden; Jeremiah 23:33,36

The Era of Jacob

The world has just ushered in the third and final era of Jacob or era of Spirit, ushering in a worldwide movement toward spiritual awareness, a time in which, according to scripture, spirit is to be poured out of God's Spirit upon all flesh. This spirit is referring to the holy spirit, which is to be poured out internally for one divine purpose— to bring us into the light of our own spirit and word. As we leave the previous era of Isaac, an era of mockery that began two thousand years ago, we find ourselves at a universal crossroads, taxed to make a choice. We can choose Esau by continuing to listen to the lies of our mind, forfeiting our spiritual birthright. Or we can choose Jacob, claiming our birthright through a process that will have us overturning the false images or beliefs we have set up on *"the fleshy tables"* in that spiritual temple called the *heart,* which Jesus illustrated for us by overturning the *tables* in the *temple.* It is in the heart or spiritual womb that we find two manner of fruit, good and evil; truth and lie.

14

And the Lord said unto her, Two nations are in thy womb, and two manner of people shall be separated from thy bowels; and the one people shall be stronger than the other people; and the elder shall serve the younger. Genesis 25:23

We choose Esau by looking outside of ourselves for salvation. Nothing that comes from the outside can save us, as it is from ourselves that we must be saved. Salvation is internal, a spiritual birthing process, which Esau rejected, forfeiting his birthright for *red pottage,* which translates to *dangerous arrogance.* It is the haughtiness of the mind's ego that has kept us from humbling ourselves to God's plan of salvation. It is the arrogance of a deluded mind that holds the holy spirit and truth hostage, keeping these two internal witnesses imprisoned, buried deep within the heart. Man has been resisting the holy spirit; the divine energy needed to give birth to the righteous word of truth from within his heart, since time began— truth that will liberate our mind, heart, and body, making us free mentally, emotionally, and physically. We choose Jacob by going within, taking a journey through our own mind and heart; a journey of deliverance that will be preceded by a mental, emotional, or physical time of trouble, as it is written, *"and there shall be a time of trouble, such as never was since there was a nation even to that same time: and at that time thy people shall be delivered…" Daniel 12:1*

The intensity of our tribulation or time of trouble depends on what it takes to motivate us to be delivered from our old way of life. What will it take to admit to ourselves that our present life is no longer working for us, to admit that our problems go a lot deeper than we thought, and cannot be solved by anything external; not by drugs, alcohol, sex, money, eating the right foods, finding the right partner, or by our current religious beliefs or spiritual practices? When we enter this humbled state we have made our way down to a symbolic

15

Jordan, where in a strong desire to change our life, our heart cries out, it's holy spirit moving upon the face of the waters, revealing the thoughts that have been hidden in the depths of our mind. When these thoughts are brought up before our face; into our mind, it exposes the dry land called earth, exposing what is in the heart. The twelve stones that were placed in the Jordan allow us to pass over into the promised land, symbolizing the good life promised us by God. We take possession of this life by driving the unholy inhabitants out of our heart, which entered in through the evil we ate of throughout our life. This duality of good and evil, symbolized by a flaming sword (Genesis 3:24), keeps us from entering back into the good life symbolized by the Garden of Eden. The word garden means protection. The word Eden means pleasant. Through the purification of our heart we renew our mind, entering a state that gives us the ability or capacity to truly enjoy our life, a life in which we find pleasure and through which we are guaranteed protection.

Take you twelve men…out of every tribe a man. And command them, saying, Take you hence out of the midst of the Jordan… twelve stones… oh and take you up every man of you a stone upon his shoulder, according unto the number of the tribes of the children of Israel.
Joshua 4:2-5

Twelve steps to claiming a more abundant life.

Chapter Three
Judging Reuben

Reuben, thou art my firstborn, my might, and the beginning of my strength, the excellency of dignity, and the excellency of power: Unstable as water, thou shalt not excel; because thou wentest up to thy father's bed; then defilest thou it: he went up to my couch. Genesis 49:3,4

Reuben, God's might, the beginning of His strength, dignity and power. *Reuben* symbolizes *our holy spirit, our portion* of God's Holy Spirit, which has been added to our physical flesh through the breath of life. No longer sustained by our mother's flesh we enter our own beginning. We have our own strength or power, our own energy or spirit, which gives our body its vitality. This spirit provides us with *dignity,* meaning *an elevation, a lifting up,* providing us with that feeling of complete self-love and acceptance, which we possessed as infants, marveling at that formed creation that is our body. We enter this world as spirit and flesh in its highest and finest degree, likened unto Adam and Eve, who in their beginning lived in an elevated spiritual state of existence. A continual dance takes place between our spirit and flesh, and there is a flowing rhythm to the dance, the spirit taking its rightful position in leading the flesh. Both the spirit and the flesh are content as we receive an abundance of love and our physical needs are met. And the dance continues…

Creation of our first heaven

But in the process of time, through the power of thought, our mind begins *an expanse,* the meaning of the word *firmament.* This is the beginning of the creation of our first heaven. *"In the beginning God created the heaven and the earth."* To create is to think in the mind, to have the idea or concept of something. Nothing has been made yet. *"And the earth was without form."* In the beginning, it was God's holy spirit that influenced the thoughts of our mind, as God's Spirit moved upon or influenced the waters. When spirit influences the thoughts of the mind there is a reaction, seen outwardly in the action of the body. The first reaction to the first thought influenced by the holy spirit of the heart was our cry, through which our physical and emotional needs were met.

In the beginning, the mind, heart, and body are working together in perfect three-part harmony. Then the mind of the infant begins to expand, and the intellect, which gives the mind the ability to reason, teaches the infant that his cry has the ability to control his external world, his parents. Through this primordial knowledge, the mind seeks its own power in order to satisfy its own agenda, which goes beyond the physical and emotional needs of the infant. This is where the ego, the personality component that is conscious, most immediately controls behavior, and is most in touch with external reality, is born. This is where the heart's what I need is overshadowed by the mind's what I want— lust.

Now there are two powers; two spirits or energies. And sound, vibration, is caused by energy. So if the parent is astute, they can determine which power is influencing the child through the sound of its cry, and respond accordingly. The rhythmic dance between holy spirit and the flesh ends when the ego or lust-driven mind begins leading the flesh. The ego, which is energetically male, is now having intercourse, communicating with the body through the mind, which are energetically female. This spiritual union marks the beginning of the creation of our first heaven, which is ready to conceive of the first of its many perceptions. Referred to as the *"lights in the firmament of the heaven"* (Genesis 1:14), these perceptions determine how we think, how we see things.

The first perception conceived of in the infant's mind will be a misconception; error with regard to the concept of love. If parents allow their infant to manipulate them through a contrived cry, which goes beyond the physical and emotional needs of the infant, they create lust in the infant, teaching them that external gratification or control equates to love. When parents, out of their own confused feelings, give in to their child's manipulation, they sanction the child's wrong perception, which is error or sin. *"Then when lust hath conceived, it bringeth forth sin"* (James 1:15). The parent's false perception of love has given life to the infant's mistaken notion of love; the first lie perceived in the child's newly formed heaven. And the negative consequence will be the formation of flesh, illustrated for us by Adam and Eve, who after listening to the serpent, symbolizing the lie, received *"coats of skins"* (Genesis 3:21), the consequence for accepting and acting upon the lie. It is a type of flesh that will limit us for the rest of our lives. The wrong thought became the false belief that caused them to take the wrong action, disobedience that separated them from their good life in the garden, as the lies of our mind become the false beliefs that we will act upon, leading to burdensome and sorrowful circumstances, separating us from an abundant and joyful life. This misconception of love is the beginning of our fall from *"the excellency of dignity and the excellency of power,"* the positive aspect of Reuben.

When a parent repeatedly gives in to the demands of their child by responding to the contrived cry, they are giving power to the lower form of desire working through the mind of the child, bringing about a shift of power in the child; the holy spirit of love giving way to the unholy spirit of lust.

If the child is taught to equate love with external gratification, he will confuse the feeling that comes with every want being satisfied, with love. And since lust is never satisfied, all the things in this world will not fill the void created in the heart of the child through this loss of divine power or holy spirit, buried in the heart of the adult child until it is lifted up, revitalized, quickened. When the lower power of the mind begins to lead the flesh body, they co-create; the lust of the flesh creating an invisible type of flesh; a sinful spiritual flesh in which another spirit, one opposing love, will breathe life.

Unstable as water, thou shalt not excel; because thou wentest up to thy father's bed: then defilest thou it: he went up to my couch. Genesis 49:4

And Israel journeyed, and spread his tent beyond the tower of Edar. And it came to pass, when Israel dwelt in that land, that Reuben went and lay with Bilhah his father's concubine.. Genesis 35:21,22

Israel symbolizes the *Mind*. The word *Edar* means *to miss or find wanting*, defining sin, lust conceived. The negative aspect of Reuben is an unholy spirit that does not allow the mind to excel, limitation brought on by the mind's journey into a false perception. The mind, once influenced by a holy spirit, has now defiled the bed of the holy spirit by communicating with another spirit, *Bilhah,* meaning *to palpitate; to terrify, be afraid.* The new spirit ruling the mind is fear; an unholy spirit that causes the mind to perceive lies as truth, mistaking darkness for light, evil for good, bringing *woe,* meaning *grief, misery.*

Woe unto them that call evil good, and good evil; that put darkness for light, and light for darkness... Isaiah 5:20

Our first heaven is one of fear and darkness, not love and light. The lies we accepted in our heart formed an invisible flesh. The spirit or energy of this flesh is fear, which is opposed to the God's Spirit, which is Love. The fear of the

20

mind, through its false perceptions, causes the mind to become unstable, unable to excel; inferior. This fearful *flesh* prevents us from doing the things we truly desire to do in this life, being contrary to the holy *spirit.* (Galatians 5:17).

When parents, out of their own fear of not being loved by their child, allow their child to control them, they teach them at the mind level that love equates to having control over their external world. When the child inevitably learns that he cannot always control his external world, he becomes fearful. In an effort to overcome this fear he will cry out all the more, an attempt to regain control over his external world. This is the perfect time for parents to drive out the lie they have caused to inhabit their child's mind. By pulling back, not allowing the manipulation or control to continue by running into the room at every little whimper, which will require them to fight against their own fear and guilt, they will restore truth in their child's mind, teaching them that controlling their external world through manipulation is not love. They will teach their child to be patient, to trust, to know that their needs will be taken care of, and that there is nothing to fear. They will reinstruct their child, teaching them the true meaning of love, and what godly love feels like, reinstating their child's holy spirit, reconciling the child's mind and heart. But unfortunately parents miss this opportunity, the child's fear taking hold, through which other negative spirits, energies, or emotions will draw power.

If a child is taught that he has the power to control his external world, he will not only become fearful when his world hits him with something he can't control, he will take on the guilt for the painful things going on around him, blaming himself if daddy leaves, or if mommy is unhappy. We must correct this misconception of love that is leading our children into fear, lies, and future sorrows, requiring discipline; a demonstration of a parent's love for his child.

He that spareth his rod hateth his son: but he that loveth him chasteneth him betimes. Proverbs 13:24

Early Mind-Heart-Body Discipline

To restore our child's holy spirit of love, bringing it back to its rightful position of leading the mind and body, will take discipline. And if we love our children, and want the positive and constructive energy of their holy spirit to lead them throughout their life, we will establish borders through the rod of discipline, *betimes,* meaning *early.* How early? With respect to the mind and heart it should be applied as soon as the child begins taking control through manipulation, playing upon his parents emotions through his cry. Picking up the child every time he cries is over-nurturing. This extending of emotional borders causes an emotional imbalance, which the child will exhibit through emotional outbursts, and through a lack of temperance with regard to his actions, all due to a lack of *early* mental, emotional, and physical restraint.

The action of mind and heart; thought and emotion, which determine the action of the body, are spiritual, and so is the rod that is to be applied to them. Disciplining the child's mind begins by curbing the manipulation taking place from that precursory restraint or discipline called the crib. But disciplining the disobedient action of the child's body is physical, taking place outside of the crib, which won't take much time and effort if the mental discipline has been consistently enforced. I salute the parents of my own generation, whose all-but-lost wisdom provided us with borders. Mental borders were established early on. Having met our physical and emotional needs, they let us cry until we exhausted ourselves and fell asleep. And I know that could not have been easy. But they held fast to the wisdom of old, and we reaped the benefits, one of which was a healthy set of lungs, not requiring the support of inhalers to simulate the breath of life; a sign pointing to a spiritual deficiency. Our physical borders came in the form of playpens, and discipline; a slap on the hand or bottom after a couple of warnings. When they said, *"This is going to hurt me more than it hurts you,"* they meant it. It must have been difficult, but they did it, overcoming their own fear, setting boundaries in the spirit of love. But today the approach is different, a result of so many parents accepting that physical discipline is wrong, that it teaches violence. Any action executed in the positive spirit of love will not produce a negative reaction. It does not teach violence, nor does it cause it. But they have accepted this lie nevertheless, and rather than establish borders in love through physical discipline, they remove the borders, putting everything out of reach of the child. They do this because they fear that if they discipline their child their child will hate them, when just the opposite is true. What the parents are actually teaching the child is that whatever is in their reach is theirs for the taking. This presents a problem for the parents when the child, entering an environment other than his own, reaches for everything in sight. It also presents a problem for the child when he enters a world full of dangerous and deadly things. If the child is not taught early on that the world consists of things that are permissible and things that are not permissible, he will lack the ability to make that distinction later on in life when he needs it the most. Sure it takes a lot more work, but the lesson will prove to be invaluable.

Keeping the boundaries narrowly defined places the child in an invisible wall of protection; in a spiritual garden. The parent can rest assure that if he establishes these mental, emotional, and physical boundaries early on that his child will remain in their safety for the rest of his life. But when parents fail to establish these borders they play a pivotal role in diminishing their child's holy spirit, compromising their child's protective internal guidance system. The child will end up making destructive choices throughout his life due to his lack of emotional well-being; an inherent quality of his holy spirit, which has been compromised due to a lack of love, which God's Word clearly tells us equates to a lack of discipline— mental, emotional, and physical, discipline.

A parent screams *"NO, STOP!"* as his child approaches the street into the path of an oncoming car. But the child doesn't stop because he has not been taught to associate his physical disobedience with a painful physical consequence. And if we fail to teach our children this important physical truth, we fail to teach them its corresponding spiritual truth, the consequence of spiritual disobedience will be spiritual or emotional pain. Discipline is God's compassionate law of love, which He set in motion from the beginning of time. When Eve disobeyed the word of God in the garden by acting on the lie, there was a painful physical consequence; the physical pain of delivery. This same law of love, which the parent teaches through a small degree of physical pain, through which the child learns empathy, will deliver the child from dangerous, and even deadly situations throughout his life. This early mind-heart-body discipline keeps the child in perfect mental, emotional, and physical balance; in perfect harmony— in one accord.

The rod of discipline is to be applied early, before the crying turns into whining, and the whining into the full-blown tantrum. Well in advance of the terrible twos; a trite expression that keeps parents from taking responsibility for the transference of power they have caused to take place in their child. If we continue to fail to execute this early three-fold discipline, we will find that we bring forth more and more children, who while seemingly higher in intelligence, are emotionally deficient. The result of an internal transference of power, which takes the power away from the heart and gives it to the mind, which seems to be acceptable, as we appear to be more impressed with IQ's (intelligence quotients) than we are with EQ's (emotional quotients). So many children today are extremely out-of-balance; an emotional imbalance stemming from a lack of mental and physical discipline. It seems we can't even find the balance when it comes to disciplining our children, disciplining them in anger or not disciplining them at all out of fear; two destructive energies. And the world's special children, who many profess to be the spiritual teachers of our world? They are in fact here to teach us an important spiritual truth, which is that we, the adults are disconnected from our emotions; emotionally detached.

God's Method of Discipline

God's way is to discipline our children early on, prior to the onset of memory. And even if the physical discipline takes place during a time that can be recalled, that memory will not carry any negative or destructive emotional energy providing the discipline was executed in the spirit of love. God reveals His method of discipline through scripture, His children given two warnings, the judgment executed upon the third infraction. This way, the discipline is performed before the parent gets angry, ensuring it is executed in the right spirit, the wisdom of God's Word.

Man's Method of Discipline

When parents began rejecting God's method of discipline they found themselves in a dilemma, forced to resort to man-made methods, such as the time out, where the parent disengages from his child mentally, emotionally, and physically. Another method, which I call emotional coercion, stands in stark contrast to God's method. Many, convinced that physical discipline is wrong, are choosing this emotional approach, taking away something the child loves as a means of controlling his behavior. Not only does it teach the child that things hold the greatest value in this life, it toys with the last vestige of the soul; the emotions. What is left for a child to trust in when the desires or joys of his heart are being used to manipulate him, to force him into obedience? And the most important question of all? How will this fear of losing what they love if they are not subordinate play out in their adolescent or adult life? If we call God's good word on disciplining our children evil; negative and destructive, what are we to call man's method of controlling their behavior, which causes emotional pain by isolating the child or by taking away something he loves, creating fear in the child. The emotions are the most sacred attribute of the soul, and should never be used to coerce the child into obedience.

He that spareth his rod hateth his son: but he that loveth him chasteneth him betimes. Proverbs 13:24

The fear that keeps many parents from disciplining their children has given power to the emotion born out of fear. According to God's Word, he that spares the rod hates his son, the *son* symbolizing the *highest state* of the soul, the vital principle in man credited to the faculty of thought, emotion, and action, kept pure through God's three-fold discipline; an act of love. This lack of love is manifesting in our children, demonstrated through a self-hatred that has them starving their bodies and cutting their flesh. Anger is born out of fear, the same fear that kept parents from establishing narrowly defined mental, emotional, and physical borders, in which the child feels safe and secure. If we return to God's method of discipline we will free our children from a prison of evil or destructive energy. And in the process, we will free ourselves from our own prison, the one we entered the day we allowed our children to have rule over us.

But lift thou up thy rod, and stretch out thine hand over the sea, and divide it: ... Exodus 14:16

By lifting up our metaphorical *rod* through the mind discipline of silence, we lift up our holy spirit, which uses its power over the *sea;* over *the thoughts hidden in the depths of our mind*, bringing them up to the surface; from the subconscious, a completely spontaneous occurrence in that it takes place through the power of the heart, not the power of the mind. We can however help facilitate the healing process by using the power of our mind to become aware of the repetitive thoughts of our mind, symbolized by the waves of the sea; those thoughts that are already at the surface, the ones that hit us over and over again. They are powerful and destructive, a product of the lower waters, which are at the root of our fears. And what influences these lower waters or seas, is the moon, the planet associated with the emotions. And the heart, which the earth symbolizes, is the seat of the emotions. So in understanding the workings of God's heaven and earth we can understand the workings of our own mind and heart, seeing how they are interconnected, influencing one another. It is to our advantage to continue the mind-body discipline of meditation and energy work throughout this healing process, which through its completion transforms the negative aspect of Reuben into the positive aspect of Reuben; *fear* into *love.*

There is no fear in love; but perfect love casteth out fear... 1 John 4:18

The word Reuben, when hyphenated, Reu-ben, reveals the shortened form of Reuben, Jacob's first son, and shortened form of Benjamin, Jacob's last son. *Reuben* means *see ye a son. Benjamin* means *a son of the right hand.* The *son* symbolizes *the highest spiritual state*, which goes from envisioning it to experiencing it through our judgment upon the meaning of Jacob's sons. The *right hand* symbolizes *power,* the holy spirit that brings truth, the spiritual seed or word of God, which once conceived by the heart, makes us a spiritual *son* of God. We resist the holy spirit of our heart by giving in to our fears

27

of our mind, which are as diverse as the lies they empower. Fighting against this unholy fear creates the doorway by which we enter into a new life. And entering into something new is always a bit scary. Look at the children of Israel, who left behind what they knew to enter into something they knew nothing about. We will fight against degrees of fear throughout this process, which begins with the fear of leaving behind our old life, illustrated by the children of Israel's exodus from Egypt, followed by a fear of confronting the hidden thoughts of our mind, symbolized by the parting of the Red Sea, followed by the fear of rising above the painful hidden emotions of our heart, which the children of Israel illustrated for us through their fear of ascending the mount. But upon completion of this marvelous process we will have fulfilled God's covenant of circumcision, the spiritual flesh of our heart removed, the veil separating our mind and heart, keeping us in darkness to ourselves, rent. This is a process that will bring us to love. Not to a selfish love driven by lust; the lower form of desire, but to a divine love, as it is written, *"love thy neighbor as thyself."* It begins with loving self!

Week 1
Acknowledging our fear

Become aware of your thoughts, those that are right at the surface, repetitive thoughts that hit you over and over again like the perpetual waves of the sea. They might come in the form of accusations or judgments; those disapproving thoughts you have about yourself, or others. What we dislike or judge in another serves to reveal what we dislike or judge in ourselves, a truth we hide from ourselves by projecting it outwardly, onto someone else. It is our familiarity with what we judge in another that gives us the ability to see it in them; *"familiar spirits,"* the Bible calls them. So become mindful of these judgments. Are they revealing the negative and destructive way you are thinking and feeling about yourself? If your negative thought is coming in the form of an accusation, look to see if you are guilty of the same thing. Are you unwittingly revealing a personal weakness or area of contention in your own life? The unholy spirit that gives power to these repetitive thoughts is fear, so attempt to deduce what that fear is.

We judge Reuben by acknowledging the fear of our mind, and by overcoming enough of this unholy fear to begin our spiritual journey. The color associated with Reuben is red.

Note: Incorporating the mind disciple of silence and energy work throughout the process will keep the positive energy of the heart flowing, and aid in the release of the negative energy bound up in the energy centers of the body. While these exercises are particularly effective during the second phase of the process, they are a benefit to the first phase as well. The first phase, works accomplished through the power of the mind, acknowledging thoughts and emotions already at the surface, will be enhanced through these mental and physical exercises. If you have already begun these exercises, you may have thoughts and feelings that are coming to you spontaneously. Being a single process, in which all the phases of the process can occur simultaneously, the heart, through the release of emotions, will be pushing thoughts and memories to the surface, which the mind has no control over. Make note of these thoughts, along with any fears you discover are associated with them.

Chapter Four
Judging Simeon & Levi

Simeon and Levi are brethren; instruments of cruelty are in their habitations. O my soul, come not thou into their secret; unto their assembly, mine honour, be not thou united: for in their anger they slew a man, and in their self-will they digged down a wall. Cursed be their anger, for it was fierce; and their wrath, for it was cruel: I will divide them in Jacob, and scatter them in Israel.   Genesis 49:5-7

The positive aspect of Reuben is the spirit of love, a creative power demonstrated through God's creation of heaven and earth, symbolizing the mind and heart. A mind that is influenced solely by the holy spirit of the heart is not subject to wrong thoughts. With only right thoughts ruling the mind, the heart is ruled by only positive emotions. But unfortunately, that's not the way it went. When we began resisting the holy spirit of our heart by accepting lies as truth, we gave power to the unholy spirit that works through our mind, fear that gives its power and strength to the many lies we speak through our mind. This negative spirit does further damage by keeping the negative and destructive thoughts or memories hidden in the darkness of denial and repression, from being seen, and what we cannot see we fear; the negative aspect of Reuben. As the sea covers the earth, these evil, negative and destructive thoughts cover our heart, the pain associated with them bringing on the birth of two more destructive energies; the negative aspects of *Simeon and Levi.*

Creation of our first earth

When we have a thought, and we focus on that thought, it becomes energized, moving out, reaching beyond the mind; beyond the heaven, reaching into the earth; into the heart, the seat of the emotions.

And the earth was without form and void... And God said, Let there be light, and there was light. Genesis 1:2, 3

When a thought affects us at a heart level, emotionally, the door of our heart opens up to receive it. The energized seed of thought, through the power of emotional energy, causes our heart to conceive of the seed, where it takes *form*. *"The seed is the word of God"* (Luke 8:11). God sowed the good seed in the earth through the power of His Holy Spirit— *"and God saw that it was good"* (Genesis 1:12). Man has sown evil seeds in his heart through the power of an unholy spirit, which was the creation of our *"first earth."*

The first word or seed to be spoken or sowed through God's Spirit, was *light*. All things are made by a seed, which is the life (John 1:2,3), and the light. Our fist earth was made by a seed; brought into existence by our word. Being gods, made in the image of God (Genesis1:27), we have the power of creation. We have spiritual energy through which we have sown spiritual seed, the two things needed for creation.

Woe unto them that call evil good, and good evil; that put darkness for light, and light for darkness... Isaiah 5:20

The good seed or word of truth, sown in the heart through the holy spirit of the heart, has us dwelling in the light, in which we make right choices, bringing positive experiences. The evil seed or word of error, sown in the heart through the unholy spirit of the heart, has us dwelling in darkness, in which we make wrong choices, bringing negative experiences, as mistaking evil for good, darkness for light, or lies for truth brings *woe*, meaning *grief; misery.*

And after they had mocked him, they took the robe off from him, and put his own raiment on him, and led him away to crucify him. And as they came out, they found a man of Cyrene, Simon by name: him they compelled to bear his cross. Matthew 27:31,32

Simon, or *Simeon* (Hebrew) demonstrates that the burden we are carrying is the consequence of our word, not God's word. God's word, the good seed, truth, makes us free. Our word, the evil seed of false beliefs, keeps us in bondage mentally, emotionally, and physically, which is bondage of the soul.

And the burden of the Lord shall ye mention no more: for every man's word shall be his burden; for ye have perverted the words of the living God, of the Lord of hosts our God. Jeremiah 23:36

Jesus carried the cross to demonstrate how *man's word* weighs heavily upon the truth, crucifying it daily from within.

And God said, Let the earth bring forth grass, the herb yielding seed, and the fruit tree yielding fruit after his kind, whose seed is in itself, upon the earth: and it was so... and God saw that it was good.
Genesis 1:11,12

As God's word made the *grass* that covers the earth, man's word has formed the *flesh* that covers the heart, as it is written, *"All flesh is grass"* (Isaiah 40:6), referring to this internal flesh. To discover the evil seed or false word that has been sown in our heart will require the release of the repressed thought or memory that has been concealing it. A thought, referred to as a seed, becomes a seed when it is sown in the heart through the power of emotion, the word *seed* meaning *something sown.* The mental effort we put into a thought energizes it, giving it a degree of power, but not enough to cause what we think in our mind to become our reality. For that to occur, the thought must become a seed, word, or belief, sowed in the heart through emotional energy. For the heart to conceive of the good seed, word, or belief, the evil seeds must first be removed, a process that transforms destructive emotional energy into creative energy, allowing the new creation to begin its formation, which will result in joyful experiences. To discover the evil seeds that have been sown in our heart we must stop resisting the holy spirit that brings the subconscious thoughts and memories, those carrying the destructive energy, into our awareness; into our conscious mind.

...Because thou hast hearkened unto the voice of thy wife, and has eaten of the tree, of which I commanded thee, saying, Thou shalt not eat of it: cursed is the ground for thy sake; in sorrow shall thou eat of it all the days of thy life; Thorns and thistles shall it bring forth to thee...

Genesis 3:17,18.

The *thorns and thistles* symbolize the *pain and aggravation* we bring into our life because we ate of the evil by accepting the lies as truth, which causes mental anguish— *sorrow*. If we continue to resist our holy spirit, which moves these negative and destructive thoughts or memories up into to our conscious mind, we will never see the destructive beliefs that exist below them, in the heart, where we will discover two more very destructive spirits.

The Destructive Spirits of the Heart and Body

Simeon and Levi are brethren; ...

If the unholy fear of the mind is not thwarted by establishing early mental, emotional, and physical boundaries, the negative thoughts of the mind will become the false beliefs of the

34

heart, sustained by painful emotions, which in time lead to destructive actions of the body.

Simeon and *Levi* are the *unholy spirits* of the *heart* and *body.* They are *brethren, kindred spirits;* where one exists, so too does the other, their relationship symbiotic. *Simeon* means *to hear intelligently (often with implication of attention, obedience, etc).* And what we hear or obey is our word, be it good or evil, truth or lie, seed that has been sown in our heart through positive or negative emotions. To hear is to believe, and to believe is to obey or put action to. Adam and Eve believed the word of the serpent, acting on it. *Levi* means *to join, to unite.* Where there is a belief, there will be an action that unites with it; that stands in support of it. If what we think is a lie, the spirit or emotion associated with it will be negative, and the action that is ruled by that emotion, destructive.

The *spirit of Levi* is the *spirit of limitation and restriction,* which the Mosaic Law, added because of disobedience, instituted by priests from the tribe of Levi, represents. When the heart of the children of Israel was bound to a false belief, which they demonstrated by worshipping the gold calf, it gave power to a law that governed their mind and body. The mind, heart, and body were in bondage, binding of the soul.

… instruments of cruelty are in their habitations. O my soul, come not thou into their secret; unto their assembly, mine honour, be not thou united:…

The *cruelty* of Simeon and Levi is the result of the unholy spirits they represent. The *habitations* of these unholy spirits are the heart and body, which in conjunction with the unholy spirit of the mind, perpetuates the destructive cycle. The *soul* is the vital principle in man credited to the faculty of thought, emotion, and action; functions of the mind, heart, and body. The *secret* of Simeon and Levi, and the *assembly* promoting it is revealed to us in the book of Genesis.

The Cruelty of Simeon and Levi

Overview: Jacob enters the city of Shechem with his daughter and twelve sons. Shechem, son of Hamor, lies with Dinah for his soul clave unto her, he loved her. But the sons of Jacob see Shechem as having defiled their sister, insisting that all the men in the city be circumcised. The men of Shechem obey. But on the third day, the men of Shechem, still weak from circumcision, are slain by Simeon and Levi, a cruel act that sorely displeased Jacob. The word *city* means *to have your eyes opened*. The word *Shechem* means *to incline the shoulder to a burden*. The word *Dinah* means *to judge*. To go into the city of Shechem is to have our eyes opened to the burden of our word. To lie with Dinah is the act of judging or overcoming that burdensome word— an act of loving our self.

When the burden of our destructive word has weighed us down long enough, we will be ready to judge or overcome it. Shechem is the son of *Hamor,* meaning *ass,* whose euphemism we want to focus on here. And who says God doesn't have a sense of humor? When we acknowledge the fact that we have made an ass out of ourselves by allowing these beliefs to rule our life, we will be ready to accept responsibility for the negative, destructive, unpleasant consequences they have brought into our life, and for the negative and destructive effects they may have had on others.

And the ass said unto Balaam, Am I not thine ass, upon which thou hast ridden ever since I was thine unto this day?... Numbers 22:30

... the dumb ass speaking with man's voice forbad the madness of the prophet. 2 Peter 2:16.

We became *the dumb ass,* a beast of burden, by accepting the false word as truth. When we acknowledge that the ass is ours; that we are the ass, we will stop the madness of the internal false prophet that has been speaking lies to us. The word *madness* means *to misthink, insanity.*

The sons of Jacob mandate circumcision for the men of Shechem, as the healing process seen through the sons of Jacob mandates spiritual circumcision; the removal of the invisible flesh formed by our word of error. When we are inclined to carry our burden by taking responsibility for what our false word has caused us to do, we become a spiritual man of Shechem, experiencing a spiritual circumcision, which is three-fold— mind, heart, and body. The removal of this spiritual flesh allows truth to penetrate our mind and heart, our third circumcision taking place when our physical body is removed or separated from our soul upon our death, allowing us to pass over from the physical realm to the spiritual realm. So why, after being obedient to this circumcision, do Simeon and Levi put the men of Shechem to death? If this symbolized a positive and constructive circumcision it would have ended in life for the men of Shechem, not death. What is this deadly circumcision?

Woe unto you scribes and Pharisees, hypocrites! Because you pay tithe of mint, and dill and cummin, but neglect the more important matters of the Law-justice, compassion, and faith. These things you ought to practise... you purify the OUTSIDE of the cup and the dish, but within, they are full of rapine and injustice... Matthew 23:23,25

The circumcision that ended in death for the men of Shechem is the removal of physical or carnal things, what religion calls flesh. Mint, symbolizing money, is offered up instead of God's spiritual sacrifices; a broken spirit and a humble heart (Psalms 51:17). Some religious devotees give up drinking and dancing, while others give up wearing jewelry, make-up, and certain clothing, which the religious *assembly* has taught them is of the flesh, sin. These are not the things that defile us. Removing them from our life is not what makes us pure. This is not the flesh that is to be removed.

Blind Pharisee, cleanse first that which is within the cup and the platter, that the outside of them may be clean also. Matthew 23:26

The *cup* symbolizes the *mind* and the *platter* symbolizes the *heart*. If we purify the thoughts of our mind and the emotions of our heart, our actions will be pure, finding a perfect, healthy balance, which is pleasing to God. Jesus ate and drank with those deemed the dregs of society, labeled a winebibber and glutton by those adhering to strict religious dietary laws, which would suggest no distinction between Jesus' behavior and the behavior of those he occasionally hung out with. What set Jesus apart from the others could not be seen, existing in the energy of his thoughts and emotions, which I believe were healed between the ages of eighteen and thirty. Twelve years, representing the spiritual judgment through which we are healed. It was those of the religious assembly that accused Jesus of carrying a burden he did not carry. Jesus was not burdened by any form of addiction!

Spiritual circumcision is the removal of spiritual things; the false images or beliefs, along with their negative and destructive energies, which fuel our addictions; bondages of excess and restraint, both of which are a loss of freedom. This religious circumcision or removal of physical things brings death, as it did with the men of Shechem. Death not only to the physical pleasures that one once took part in, but death to one's soul, as the spiritual circumcision that brings life to the soul is left undone. *"O my soul, come not thou into their secret; unto their assembly."* Take no part in this religious circumcision, which is Simeon and Levi's *secret* as this type of carnal circumcision removes the physical things, but leaves the spiritual things that need to be removed, *hidden.* Spiritual circumcision removes the spiritual flesh, allowing the light of truth to penetrate our heart, exposing what is still in darkness.

Behold, thou desirest truth in the inward parts: and in the hidden part thou shalt make me to know wisdom... The sacrifices of God are a broken spirit: a broken and a contrite heart... Psalms 51:6,17.

38

The men of Shechem were weakened as a result of this circumcision as we weaken ourselves spiritually when we use the power of our mind to control or abstain from the physical pleasure, when we should be using the power of our heart to clean up the inside; wasted energy.

"Even so ye outwardly appear righteous unto men, but within ye are full of hypocrisy and iniquity" Matthew 23:28

Jesus is speaking to those of the religious assembly, which advocates for this type of carnal outward circumcision, leaving the spiritual circumcision of the heart undone.

Simeon and Levi slew the men of Shechem on the third day. *"One day is with the Lord as a thousand years"* (2 Peter 3:8). We are in the third day; in the beginning of the third thousandth year since the coming of Jesus, who taught spiritual circumcision of the heart. It is time to end this carnal circumcision that removes what the religious assembly is in great error calling flesh, and commence with spiritual circumcision, removing the flesh or foreskin of our heart by removing our false word; the false beliefs that formed the flesh that keeps us in bondage, unable to enjoy the physical pleasures that were put on this earth for us to enjoy in the spirit of moderation due to our impure spiritual state. The greatest gift God could impart to His human Adam was the gift of enjoying the physical realm with all of its visual and tactile delights; the privilege of frequently indulging in sensual gratification, but in a perfected state; with a pure mind and heart. Living the 3rd dimension, but under the divine spiritual attributes of the 5th dimension.

The Two Deadly Spirits of Simeon and Levi

for in their anger they slew a man, and in their self-will they digged down a wall...

The two unholy spirits of the heart and body are *anger* and *self-will*, the latter being excessive or lack of control with regard to our actions. It is a will that carries a very different energy than that of divine will. When the mental and physical borders of a child are not narrowly defined early on, the child is left with the idea that he has the control. If the parent attempts to regain control over the child, the child will react in anger in order to maintain control. But there is another reason for the anger he is demonstrating. If mental and physical boundaries are not established early through the rod of discipline, the child's thoughts and actions will not carry the protection that comes by remaining in those borders. His mind will be an open door to the fear associated with not having control over the painful things taking place around him, the emotional energy of that pain serving to transform the wrong thought the child is having at the time into a false belief, which he will later act upon.

The first response to the false word being accepted in the heart is *anger*, the heart's natural response that reveals how the heart feels about the evil seed that has been sown in her, choking out the good seed or word of truth. Had we known what was taking place we could have transformed this anger by using it constructively, which Jesus illustrated by turning over the images set up in the temple, symbolizing the false beliefs we have set up in that spiritual temple called the heart. The *fear* of our mind kept us from seeking the truth, giving power to the lie that would be accepted into our heart, which in turn gave power to the destructive *anger* of the heart. And what joins itself to this anger is *self-will*; a destructive *control*, a response to *fear*, perpetuating the destructive cycle. This unholy spirit of control, working through the power of the mind, is what causes us to resist the holy spirit or power of our heart, which brings us into the light of our false beliefs, whose negative energy empowers our destructive behaviors.

Through the power of truth we are made free, our *self-will* transformed into *divine will,* providing us with a balanced control called temperance; a fruit of the Spirit. No longer bound by the law of self-will or restraint, which we instituted through the power of our mind, we can enjoy the pleasures of this life without the burden of addiction, or fear thereof. Lack of control and excessive control are both addictions, serving to numb the pain and mask the anger of the heart, keeping secret how we truly feel. We use this control to control our emotions, denying ourselves permission to feel. Excessive control can be far more dangerous than lack of control, which viewed as a weakness gains quicker realization. Excessive control, often viewed as strength, is oftentimes ignored, gaining momentum through its deception, hiding what it truly is— an addiction.

When our mind is ruled by fear, and our heart is ruled by a false belief, we are in conflict with our true spiritual essence, which is love and truth— our authentic self. The negative and destructive response to this internal conflict is anger and an overpowering need for control. And thinking we have everything under control is a deception that only empowers the addiction, wreaking havoc on our body as the destructive energy contained in our hidden thoughts and emotions moves out, manifesting as pain, inflammation, tumors, cysts, disease, etc. Our protection comes by doing the heart work!

But let every man prove his own work, and then shall he have rejoicing in himself alone, and not in another: For every man shall bear his own burden. Galatians 6:4,5

When the children of Israel left Egypt, they took only their dough and kneading troughs with which to make *bread,* meaning *to overcome.* It is going to take all of our energy just to overcome our own burden. We need to lighten our load to complete this journey, which we do by letting those around us carry their own burden. When we put energy into trying to fix, save, or carry them, we weaken ourselves, depleting the energy we need for our own delivery. But when we relinquish this non-effective control through which we try to change them, we actually gain an effective control. When we stop putting our energy into trying to correct or control their negative behavior, we stop carrying their burden, putting the burden back on them, where it belongs. By no longer enabling them, we force them to take responsibility for their own negative and destructive behavior, forcing them to do their own work, through which they gain the strength they need for their own delivery. This is an act of love, toward our self, and toward them.

for in their anger they slew a man, and in their self-will they digged down a wall...

It was the *anger* of the religious assembly that *slew* the ultimate *man* of Shechem, who instructed us to carry our burden by carrying the cross. They were angry because they did not want to give up their beliefs, the pagans subject to their many gods, the Jews to their many laws. They had become addicted to their ritualistic practices and sacrifices, and yielding to the teachings of Jesus would surely take away their fix. They had become addicted to the mind peace one acquires through any practice that requires only the action of the mind and body. They held to the traditions of their fathers, offering up perpetual prayers and sacrifices, serving God with their mind and body instead of establishing authentic peace through the transformation of their heart, continuing to worship their man-made gods, and to keep the letter of the law.

And Jesus said, Are ye also yet without understanding? Do not ye yet understand, that whatsoever entereth in at the mouth goeth into the belly, and is cast out into the draught? But those things which proceed out of the mouth come forth from the heart; and they defile the man.
Matthew 15:16-18

What comes out of our mouth, which speaks for our mind, comes from the false beliefs of our heart. Instead of allowing God's word of truth to make us free of our law of control, we crucify it, choosing to obey our word of error, remaining in bondage to our old beliefs as they did two thousand years ago. And after 70 years, in 70AD, the *wall* of Jerusalem was brought down, illustrating the loss of our spiritual wall of protection, and our physical wall of protection through the premature death of our body. Life beyond 70 is called grace. This anger and control, which feeds off the fear, slays us, destroying our quality of life by removing the mental, emotional, and physical freedom to enjoy its pleasures. The *wall* that Simeon and Levi *digged* down symbolizes the protection we lose when we allow the anger of our heart and the control of our body to remain, unholy spirits that lead to disease, addiction, and compulsions.

Simeon and Levi, instruments of cruelty, seen in some of the most prevalent infirmities of our time— anorexia, bulimia, cutting, etc. What cruelty we inflict upon our bodies out of this hidden anger born out of fear, giving us a desperate need to control what is external. Fear → anger → control → fear. Without control over external things we feel powerless, and we feel powerless because we have resisted the holy power of our heart, being taught from infancy that to control our external world is love. So the external things we want, thinking they will fulfil us, never do, because the power through which we control or obtain them is not love, but lust, which is never satisfied. To transform the lust of self will back to the love of divine will is going to take some deep internal work.

From whence come wars and whence contentions among you? Come they not hence, even of your lusts that war in your members? You strongly desire, and have not, you kill, and are envious, and are not able to obtain; you fight and war. You have not because you do not ASK;

43

you ask and do not receive, because you ask wickedly, so that you may waste it on your lusts. James 4:1-3

The *members* are our *mind and heart,* where we seek to satisfy the *lusts* that are driven by the mental and emotional energy of the flesh formed by our false perceptions and beliefs. A strong desire for the things that will make us happy is a good thing. But if we draw the things we hope for through the wrong energy it will most likely turn into a bad thing, having a negative consequence, which is why it's been said, *"watch what you ask for, you just might get it."* The negative and destructive energy born out of our fear of never having it, our anger for not having received it, our need to control it, and our impatience to get it is going to end in sorrow. But if we take the time to identify and remove any error in the way we think and feel about what it is we desire, identifying our motivation for wanting it, our request will be backed by the positive energy of truth, drawing to us that which is positive, bringing us joy.

Whatsoever ye shall ask the Father in my name, he will give it you. Hitherto have ye asked nothing in my name: ask, and ye shall receive, that your joy may be full. John 16:23,24

To *ask in my name* is to *ask in truth.* We ask in truth, receiving of the joy that comes from receiving of the Father by identifying and overcoming the false belief we have with regard to what it is we desire. Otherwise, we are asking from the unholy spirit of lust, the energy of the lie or false belief, instead of from the holy spirit of love, the energy of truth, receiving the reward of pain and sorrow from a very different father. The false word of our heart, fueled by the unholy spirits of anger and control, plays over and over again through the fearful and controlling thoughts of our mind, perpetuating an endless cycle of unhealthy behaviors. These

44

beliefs act as internal tyrants, berating and humiliating us, making us feel like we aren't good enough or don't measure up. But if we bring down the false beliefs driving our destructive behaviors there will be no destructive anger to drive us to inflict this dangerous, excessive or lack of control over our body, ending the vicious cycle.

Identifying our anger

Do we become angry when we are ridiculed? Do we become angry when we are corrected or confronted for our actions? Does our anger rise up when we find we are not able to control ourselves, someone else, or a particular situation? Do we allow someone else's anger to trigger our own anger? Is our anger directed toward our self? There will be times when the reason for our anger seems to be quite superficial, so go beneath the obvious by recalling your thoughts and feelings prior to the anger, which will lead to the bullet behind the smoking gun; the false belief behind the anger. If you are unable to identify a particular thought or feeling, make note of the person to whom the anger was directed, and to the particular situation. This will bring you one step closer to identifying the source of your anger. Becoming aware of your thoughts prior to the anger will allow you to identify other negative emotions that are related to this unholy spirit. If you discover that your anger is related to jealousy, make note of it. These spirits are what the Bible refers to as *"familiar spirits,"* and how these spirits came to be so familiar to us can be found in the word's derivative, *familia,* Latin for FAMILY. We took possession of these spirits through the painful things we saw, heard, felt, and experienced in our family. By keeping a list of the spirits or emotions associated with our anger, seeing which ones keep repeating, and how often, we will be able to flush out the false word or belief, which is something we accepted as truth, but which was in fact a lie, having a negative, destructive, unpleasant, or undesirable outcome.

Identifying our will — self or divine?

If we want to know if our will is positive; coming from a loving, kind, and compassionate place, or negative; coming from a fearful, angry, and cruel place, all we have to do is relinquish our control by breaking one of our self-imposed laws. Do we become fearful? Do we feel anxious? Do we get angry with ourselves? Do we get depressed? Do we beat ourselves up about it? Do we immediately enact an even stiffer law to compensate for our failure to keep our self-imposed law? If we can answer yes to any of these questions it is self-will, a control instituted through the power of the mind. How often do we set up a rule or law in our mind in order to control the action of our body? In what areas do we deny ourselves pleasure, or over-indulge in pleasure. We are looking for both sides of this self-will. In what areas of our life do we plunge ahead without thinking, or shrink back in fear? This control is connected to our anger, which will lead to us to discovering the false word or belief of our heart, which has continued to control our life, yet has managed to go undiscovered for all these years.

Fear may have us obsessing about the food as it enters our mouth. Fearful of the effects we think the food is having upon our body we impose a stiff law that severely restricts our food intake; the excessive control of the destructive disorder anorexia. Over-indulgence or abstinence with regard to food is simply a way of dealing with painful emotions through the process of eating. Why is it that some can consume small amounts of food and gain weight, while others can eat considerable amounts of food and not gain a pound? This has been chalked up to genetics. But what really determines our genetic coding? We have come to accept that many of our disorders, diseases, and addictions are hereditary. But in truth, it is not the disorder, disease, or addiction that is handed down, but a way of thinking, feeling, and believing; mental and emotional energy that manifests as the disorder, disease, or addiction. It all boils down to the thoughts of our mind and the feelings of our heart; a parental legacy passed down from generation to generation, a spiritual inheritance written in the will of those that came before us. But we need not accept their will as our own, each of us possessing the power to hold on to what has been passed down, or dump it.

I will divide them in Jacob, and scatter them in Israel. Genesis 49:7

The sons of Jacob are the tribes of Israel (Genesis 49:28), which were divided through inheritance. Three of these tribes received their inheritance east of the Jordan. They helped fight against the inhabitants of the Promised Land, but did not remain there. Reuben, Simeon, and Levi parallel the three tribes that helped take possession of the Promised Land, as acknowledging our fear, anger, and control will help us in our battle to take possession of a new life.

When we discover the belief generating our anger and need for control, and then go through the process of transforming that belief, we will find that the negative behavior of others no longer affects us in quite the same way. We will find that our reaction is quite different. Having rid ourselves of the destructive anger through the elimination of the false belief, we also rid ourselves of the destructive control. Our new reaction is that of divine will, a new control. The power of truth, which if not rejected, will effect positive change in those receiving it, whose bad behavior we once enabled through our old control, which generated by fear and fueled by anger only allowed them to justified their negative and destructive behavior. But now, having *"no cloke for their sin,"* they can come face to face with their own sin, an opportunity

47

to see and overcome the error they are still holding on to. This new control or divine will ensures that we no longer contribute to empowering the spiritual and physical addictions of those we love, which we helped perpetuate through our own addiction to unholy fear, anger, and control. When we end the fear → anger → control → fear cycle in ourselves, we contribute to the potential for others to end it in themselves— a demonstration of love from both sides.

Week 2
Acknowledging our anger and control

Become aware of your feelings; of your anger, and the circumstances that caused this anger to come to the surface. Become aware of actions that are a direct response to this anger. Be aware of your motivation. These internal works will help you discover the cause of these two unholy spirits that inhabit your spiritual promised land, allowing you to drive them out.

We judge Simeon and Levi by acknowledging that it is our word that burdens us; false beliefs that generate this anger and control, which we either internalize or externalize. And by acknowledging that salvation comes not by removing the external things, but the internal things; the fear, anger and control that is keeping our mind, heart and body in bondage; in a mental, emotional, and physical prison.

Chapter Five
Judging Judah

Judah, thou art he whom thy brethren shall praise: thy hand shall be in the neck of thine enemies; thy father's children shall bow down before thee. Judah is a lion's whelp: from the prey, my son, thou art gone up: he stooped down, he crouched as a lion, and as an old lion; who shall rouse him up? The scepter shall not depart from Judah, nor a lawgiver from between his feet, until Shiloh come; and unto him shall the gathering of the people be. Binding his foal unto the vine, and his ass's colt unto the choice vine; he washed his garments in wine, and his clothes in the blood of grapes: His eyes shall be red with wine, and his teeth white with milk.

Genesis 49:8-12

Judah was the tribe raised up above all the other tribes. It was the tribe called out to bear the name, which was to be carried up to Jerusalem. As the tribes that made up the kingdom of Israel decreased, the kingdom of Judah increased. These two kingdoms represent our two internal kingdoms; the kingdom of heaven or realm of the mind and the kingdom of God or realm of the Heart. The transference of power from Israel to Judah reveals an internal transference of power; from the thoughts of our mind to the feelings of our heart. Judah, in the healing process, is the point at which we pass over from the darkness of ignorance or denial to the light of understanding and acceptance.

Judah, thou art he whom thy brethren shall praise: ...

The word *praise* means *a hand (indicating power) to revere or worship*. It is the feelings of the heart that the thoughts of the mind revere or worship.

thy hand shall be in the neck of thine enemies; thy father's children shall bow down before thee…

The *hand* symbolizes *power,* which is in the spirit and word of the heart, be it God's spirit and word or man's spirit and word, *thy father's children* being *Israel,* which bows down to *Judah,* as the thoughts of our *Mind* are subject to the feelings and beliefs of our *Heart.* So even if we do the work of replacing our conscious negative and destructive thoughts with positive and constructive thoughts, we still have the negative and destructive energy of our suppressed emotions. If we deny, ignore, or repress the memory, resisting the holy spirit that is bringing it to our remembrance, we will retain the painful emotions attached to it.

Judah is not just a son of Jacob, or a kingdom that came into existence under the reign of Solomon. It is an era that began two thousand years ago when God's Spirit and Word took on bodily form in John and Jesus. John preceded Jesus, as the Spirit precedes the Word, which if not resisted, will expose our word of error, and sow God's word of truth, which in turn, transforms our emotional energy.

And the Spirit of God moved upon the waters. And God said...

The *waters* symbolize the *people,* as well as the *thoughts* of their mind. The spirit of John the Baptist moved upon the people, motivating them. He preached a mind discipline, *repentance,* meaning *to think differently.* But to change the way we think so we are no longer subject to the law of self-will, having to continually control our negative and destructive thoughts through the power of our mind, will require us to sacrifice the source of these *evil thoughts.*

For out of the heart proceed evil thoughts... Matthew 15:19

For as he thinketh in his heart, so is he... Proverbs 23:7

To renew our mind will require us to sacrifice the old spirit that has been ruling our heart, influencing our thoughts in a negative way (Psalms 51:17). Through this spiritual sacrifice we revitalize the holy spirit of our heart (Psalms 51:10), which will influence our thoughts in a positive way

Judah is a lion's whelp, from the prey, my son, thou art gone up: he stooped down, he crouched as a lion, and as an old lion; who shall rouse him up? ...

Judah is an *old lion*, symbolizing an *old spirit*, which has been with us for a very long time. We have been its prey, feeding it with the food that is our word of error. But we have what it takes to slay this old *lion*.

And David said unto Saul, Thy servant kept his father's sheep, and there came a lion, and a bear, and took a lamb out of the flock. And I went out after him, and smote him, and delivered it out of his mouth; and when he arose against me, I caught him by his beard, and smote him, and slew him. 1 Samuel 17:34,35

The word *David* means *to love*, love being the holy spirit that will slay the *lion*, symbolizing the *unholy spirit*, and the *bear*, symbolizing the *unrighteous word* that lives within our heart. The bear devours much flesh, demonstrating the destructive behavior associated with our word of error, which will destroy the body before its natural time. The *lamb* symbolizes the *righteous word* of the heart, truth, which our own spirit and word are out to destroy. The word *beard* means *to be old*, revealing once again that this is an old spirit. To slay it we must first identify it through its characteristics. It is an earthly spirit, having four components. The first component, and origin, is fear. Added to this fear is anger and control. To see

51

the fourth component, let us return to Mount Sinai and let our greatest spiritual teachers, the children of Israel, show us.

And when the people saw that Moses delayed to come down out of the mount, the people gathered themselves together unto Aaron, and said unto him, Up, make us gods, which shall go before us; for as for this Moses, the man that brought us up out of the land of Egypt, we wot not what is become of him. Exodus 32:1

The last component of our own spirit is impatience. It is from these four: fear, anger, control, and impatience, that all the other unholy spirits or negative emotions get their power. These four, the negative aspects of the first four sons of Jacob, make up the lion that only love can slay. Looking back on our life, how many ways can we see that we failed to love ourselves because of the spirit of impatience? As children and teenagers, we were in a hurry to grow up instead of enjoying the innocence of our youth, indulging in adult behaviors way too soon because we feared that if we didn't we wouldn't be loved or accepted. As adults we impatiently sought a lover or spouse out of a fear of being alone. Maybe we were impatient when it came to having children, fearing the tick-tock of the biological clock, or when it came to climbing the ladder of success, compromising our integrity in the process. The spirit of impatience, working in conjunction with fear, anger, and control, is the same unholy spirit that has religious Christians proclaiming they are born of the spirit before they have gone through the process that transforms flesh into spirit. We must not get impatient when it comes to this process. Like *wine,* symbolizing *spirit,* it takes time for the flesh of the grape to be changed to wine. It's not done in a day, or twenty-eight days. Birth is a laborious process, never to be rushed! The struggle between our holy spirit and unholy spirit is will continue throughout the process. But we can lend our support by being fully aware of the characteristics of our unholy spirit. When you feel that surge of energy that is spirit, look to see if there is any element of fear, anger, control, or impatience beneath it. If you are not sure where this energy is coming from, step back from the action this spirit or energy is driving you to take, and see what feelings come up. Do you feel anxious? Do you feel any fear from stepping back and not doing what this energy is driving you to do? Do you feel angry? The anger will be coming from the false word or belief, joined by a desperate need for control. Do you feel any self-hatred, condemnation, or guilt accompanying your decision not to do what this spirit is driving you to do? If you can answer yes to any of these questions you are experiencing the different components of your unholy spirit, which lives through the negative and destructive thoughts, emotions, and beliefs, still hidden in your heart.

Impatience in the Wilderness

When the children of Israel made their way out of Egypt and into the wilderness, it was the spirit of impatience that fueled their desire to return to their old life. They preferred the bondage of Egypt over the freedom that lay just ahead. The energy of bondage still existed, transferred from a land to a law. This physical law of bondage, added because of their transgression of God's spiritual law, symbolized their spiritual law of bondage; their addiction to fear, anger, control and impatience. When we take our leap of faith by deciding to leave behind a life that has become too hard, painful, restrictive, or unfulfilling, we must continue to have faith after the leap, which is where the Israelites failed. They got out there and became fearful, which led to their constant complaining, and impatience, their rough time in the wilderness serving to prove them; to see what their intentions were. If we are serious about changing our life, if our desire is coming from our heart and not our head, then it is to the source of that desire that we must prove our loyalty. Let's face it; we haven't had the best track record when it comes to the holy spirit, which Moses symbolized, always resisting it, pushing it aside in favor of our own destructive spirit. Can we blame the holy spirit for wanting to see what our intention is? Are we going to allow ourselves to be overcome with fear, speaking our own word, which is speaking through our mind saying, *"I can't do this!"* If that is our position, then we have already sabotaged our holy spirit, which opposes fear and doubt. But if we hang in there, show intent, we will begin to see positive results. We must trust our internal God-source, do the works, and be patient!

Slaying the lion of Judah

How do we go about slaying this spirit we have given life to? We might start by looking at its four components and see how they have ruled our life. How many times have we thought about doing something but declined out of fear? How many times have we suppressed the anger of our heart, suppressing our feelings instead of expressing them, or expressing our anger through acts of rage without a thought as to why? How many times have we enacted an internal or external law of either type of control in order to feel better about ourselves, or to numb ourselves to the pain? And last but not least, how many times have we shown ourselves to be impatient, causing us to be unthankful and feeling discontent. Impatience is a dangerous spirit, which will have us skipping over the very important internal work that serves to fill the void we impatiently, and unsuccessfully try to fill with external things. The feelings that accompany our unholy spirit are anxiety and unrest, the reason for insomnia. The feelings that accompany our holy spirit are tranquility and peace, *Shiloh,* a state we enter when we overcome the four-pronged unholy spirit of Judah.

The sceptre shall not depart from Judah, nor a lawgiver from between his feet, until Shiloh come...

The word *sceptre* means *a scion, i.e a stick for punishing,* which for Israel was the *law*, representing the law of punishment we impose upon ourselves when we resist the holy spirit by giving in to the fear of our mind, as the Israelites resisted Moses, their minds overcome with an unholy fear. It is when we are separated from the *holy spirit,* as the children of Israel were separated from *Moses,* that we fall prey to the spirit of impatience, which feeds off our fear, causing us to build false images to worship, as the children of Israel built and worshipped the gold calf. The *feet* symbolizes the *age of Pisces,* an astrological sign heading each era. Aries headed the era of Abraham or Israel, which began four thousand years ago. Pisces headed the era of Isaac or Judah, which began two thousand years ago. The world has passed over into the final era of Jacob or era of Spirit, in which we are to take part in a spiritual baptism, being immersed in truth, our eyes opened to the burden caused by our false perceptions and beliefs.

Binding his foal unto the vine, and his ass's colt unto the choice vine; he washed his garments in wine, and his clothes in the blood of grapes:

The word *foal* means *opening the eyes and bearing a burden.* The burden we've been carrying, and are to have our eyes opened to, is tied to the *vine,* symbolizing a *false truth.* Accepting this false word as truth was our *choice,* which we made in the darkness of naivety. But now we see it, obligating us to bear our burden by doing something about it. Up until this point we have *washed our garments in wine,* attempting to *purify ourselves through our own spirit,* immersing ourselves in the *blood of grapes,* symbolizing *a partial processing,* faith without works, which will not make clean our robe of spiritual flesh. To turn our flesh to spirit, as grapes are turn to wine, will require us to complete God's healing or purification process.

His eyes shall be red with wine, which is to be drunk on *our own spirit. …and his teeth white with milk.*

Milk is for children, those *unskillful* in the spiritual works of God's Word. Eating *meat* is accepting truth in our heart through the application of these spiritual works— a process.

For everyone that useth milk is unskilful in the word of righteousness: for he is a babe. But strong meat belongeth to them that are of full age, even those who by reason of use have their senses exercised to discern both good and evil. Hebrews 5:13,14

Skill comes from doing the work of separating the good from the evil; the truth from the lies, the wheat from the chaff. Through our obedience to, and completion of the spiritual *works,* we receive the good *word* of truth, the holy seed, which brings forth *a son— a god.*

Is it not written in your law, I said, ye are gods. If he called them gods unto whom the word of God came, and the scripture cannot be broken; Say ye of him, whom the Father hath sanctified, and sent into the world, Thou blasphemest; because I said, I am the Son of God? If I do not the works of my Father, believe me not. But if I do, though you believe not me, believe the works:… John 10:34-38

It is through these internal works that we sacrifice our word of false beliefs, other gods, obeying God's Commandment. *"Thou shall have no other gods before me."*

For according to the number of thy cities were thy gods, O Judah...
Jeremiah 11:13

We judge Judah by becoming aware of our impatience, seeing our own spirit and word, and by continuing the process through which will overcome the four characteristics of the unholy spirit of Judah, giving power to God's spirit and word. The color associated with Judah is orange.

Chapter Six
Judging Zebulun & Issachar

Zebulun shall dwell at the haven of the sea; and he shall be for a haven of ships; and his border shall be unto Zidon. Genesis 49:13

The word *Zebulun* means *a habitation, reside, dwell with,* referring to the mind's ability to become a habitation for thoughts— memory. The *sea* symbolizes the *thoughts hidden in the depths of our mind;* hidden so deep in our psyche that most of us are still unaware of their existence. The mind's ability to store these thoughts provides a *haven,* meaning *to cover,* the mind serving as a wall of protection, behind which our negatively charged thoughts or memories find refuge. Some are right at the surface, coming in waves. But it is the deeper ones, those still in darkness to us, that are causing the lion's share of our problems. It is through the quieting of our mind that we activate the holy spirit of our heart, which moves these deeper hidden thoughts up into our consciousness.

Zebulun shall dwell at the haven of the sea; ...

The word *haven* also means *a cove, sheltered bay, shore, sea-side,* the shore being where the land or earth and sea meet, illustrating the connection between the feelings of our heart and the thoughts of our mind, the physical land of Zebulun situated, geographically, along the seaside.

Through our judgment or discernment of the first three sons of Jacob we gain insight with regard to our fear, anger, and control, making our way down to a symbolic Jordan, our mind immersed in the *great light* of truth.

The land of Zebulun and the land of Naphtali, by the way of the sea, beyond Jordan, Galilee of the Gentiles; The people which sat in darkness saw great light, and to them which sat in the region and shadow of death light is sprung up. From that time Jesus began to preach, and to say, Repent: for the kingdom of heaven is at hand. Matthew 4:15-17

The *Jordan* symbolizes *a humbled state.* When we enter this state we become a spiritual *Gentile,* which is *to be open-minded,* willing to learn about ourselves. Our mind, whose wall served to separate us from the feelings of our heart, is now being influenced by the heart. The holy spirit of our heart, no longer being resisted, can now bring the painful memories from our past up into our awareness, moving us out of *darkness* and into the *light.*

In him was life; and the life was the light of men. John 1:4

The *shadow of death* is removed by the *life* of light. Truth is light, inherent in the process of transformation. *Repent* means *to think differently,* which takes place in the *kingdom of heaven;* in the *realm of the mind.* But to change the negative and destructive way we think and behave forever we must change the negative way we feel through the transformation of our heart, which begins at Zebulun, the point at which we begin to experience those *"aha"* moments; when we begin to associate the wrong or negative way we think and feel about certain things with painful experiences from our past.

and he shall be for a haven of ships; ...

The *ship* symbolizes the *mind,* where we repress the memories that keep us bound to the suppressed emotions of our heart.

And his border shall be unto Zidon.

The word *Zidon* means *to lie along side in wait (as in the sense of catching fish), to catch an animal (fig. men), to victual (for a journey).*

And Jesus, walking by the sea of Galilee, saw two brethren, Simon called Peter, and Andrew his brother, casting a net into the sea: for they were fishers. And he said unto them, Follow me, and I will make you fishers of men. Matthew 4:18,19

Jesus told his apostles that he would make them fishers of men, and that's precisely what we will do here at Zebulun. We are going to enter our ship; that vessel called the mind, where the journey begins, and lie in wait to catch the false perceptions that rule our mind, and our life, which are coming from the false beliefs that rule our heart.

The Lights of Heaven

And God said, Let there be lights in the firmament of the heaven to divide the day from the night; and let them be for signs, and for seasons, and for days, and years: And let them be for lights in the firmament of the heaven to give light upon the earth: and it was so. And God made two great lights; the greater light to rule the day, and the lesser light to rule the night: he made the stars also. And God set them in the firmament of the heaven to give light upon the earth, And to rule over the day and over the night, and to divide the light from the darkness: and God saw that it was good. Genesis 1:14-18

The sun, moon, and stars are the *lights of heaven,* symbolizing the *perceptions of the mind,* which give *light upon the earth,* as the *heart* receives the spiritual light of understanding through these three sources, whether that light be truth, or iniquity disguised as truth, as it is written, *"And no marvel; for Satan himself is transformed into an angel of light"* (2 Corinthians 11:14).

...Behold, I have dreamed a dream more; and, behold, the sun and the moon and the eleven stars made obeisance to me. And he told it to his father, and to his brethren: and his father rebuked him, and said unto him, What is this dream that thou hast dreamed? Shall I and thy mother and thy brethren indeed come to bow down ourselves to thee to the earth? Genesis 37:9,10

The *sun* symbolizes *our father,* the *moon* symbolizes *our mother,* and the *stars* symbolize *our siblings,* relatives, or anyone else that influenced our thinking. Our light or truth came through these three sources, be it positive or negative, constructive or destructive, good or evil, every seed after its own kind.

Woe unto them that call evil good, and good evil; that put darkness for light, and light for darkness;.... Isaiah 5:20

The word *woe* means *grief, misery,* the consequence of mistaking evil for good, darkness for light; the consequence of mistaking lies for truth.

For my thoughts are not your thoughts, neither are your ways my ways, saith the Lord. Isaiah 55:8

But we will align our thoughts and ways with God's when the false perceptions that came through our metaphorical sun, moon, and stars bow down to Joseph, which takes place when these false perceptions submit to truth.

for the day of the Lord is near in the valley of decision. The sun and the moon shall be darkened, and the stars shall withdraw their shining.
Joel 3:15

The day of the Lord is to the individual, arriving *when truth comes.* Jesus returns spiritually; *in the clouds of heaven— in the thoughts of the mind.* The word *valley* means *a depression; a humble state,* in which we make the *decision* to change our life for the better.

60

Immediately after the tribulation of those days shall the sun be darkened, and the moon shall not give her light, and the stars shall fall from heaven... Matthew 24:29

This internal process begins with *tribulation,* or as the prophet Daniel put it, *"a time of trouble, such as never was"* (Daniel 12:1). For those that seek truth early, this tribulation will more likely be spiritual; mental or emotional. It may come as a feeling of unrest, or contempt for the life we have made for ourselves, followed by a great desire to leave this old way of life in search of a better way of life, as Abraham left the land of Chaldea in search of the Promised Land.

The *sun* and the *moon* are darkened, the negative influences from our *father* and our *mother* lessened in degree through our awareness of the negative and destructive traits we inherited from them; a less-than-holy spiritual inheritance. The power of these destructive thoughts and feelings, born out of what we saw, heard, felt, and experienced, will be lessened in degree, darkened, eclipsed by the light of truth as we begin to understand that we have taken on their perceptions, which they most likely took on from their parents. We begin to understand why we think, feel, and act as we do; causing us to make the choices we have throughout our life. This is not about pointing the finger of blame. It's about seeing our self, although passing through blame is part of the process that leads to true forgiveness. The *sun* also symbolizes the *ego,* which must be overshadowed if we are to begin this process. The *moon,* symbolizing the *emotions,* must also concede, which takes place when the power of painful emotions are brought into the healing light of awareness by way of our holy spirit.

Verily I say unto you, Except ye be converted, and become as little children, ye shall not enter into the kingdom of heaven. Whosoever therefore shall humble himself as a little child, the same is the greatest in the kingdom of heaven. Matthew 18:3,4

We become *as a little child* by humbling ourselves, allowing our holy spirit to take us back to our childhood, where we took on the false perceptions that became false beliefs through the power of emotion; through the fearful, hurtful, or painful things we experienced— a totally spontaneous life-review.

Verily I say unto you, Whosoever shall not receive the kingdom of God as a little child, he shall not enter therein. Mark 10:15

The *kingdom of God* symbolizes the *realm of the Heart.*

The perceptions of our mind mirror the beliefs of our heart, an awareness that comes by judging Zebulun, a land situated on the seashore, where the sea meets the earth; where we make a connection between the thoughts of our mind and the feelings and beliefs of our heart.

...YET ONCE MORE I SHAKE NOT THE EARTH ONLY, BUT ALSO HEAVEN. And this word, Yet once more, signifying the removing of those things which are shaken, as of things that are made, that those things which cannot be shaken may remain.
Hebrews 12:26, 27

Through this spiritual, mental and emotional, healing process, our *"first heaven,"* created through false perceptions, is shaken, our mind feeling unsettled as we begin to see the reality of our life, and of our world, serving to change our perceptions. Our earth shakes when the painful emotions sustaining the false beliefs of our heart are spontaneously released. When our unrighteous word; the false beliefs that inhabits our heart are shaken and released, that which cannot be shaken, the righteous word of truth, remains.

And the children of Israel did eat manna forty years, until they came to a land inhabited; they did eat manna, until they came unto the borders of the land of Canaan. Exodus 16:35

The children of Israel ate manna in the *wilderness*, symbolizing the *mind*. The word *manna* means *what? how? why? when?*, referring to the questions we will be asking ourselves in our mind.

To him that overcometh will I give to eat of the hidden manna...

The *hidden manna* is the *bread of life,* the word *bread* meaning *to overcome.* We eat of this bread from heaven when we begin to question the life we have made for ourselves. The answers we receive will be the means by which we overcome all that was negative in our life, turning our sorrow into joy.

The children of Israel ate of the manna in the literal sense, but not in the spiritual sense, refusing to question the condition of their heart, *a land inhabited* with unholy things. When they entered the *land* of Canaan, symbolizing the *heart,* they were to drive out the seven nations, symbolizing the spiritual impurities of the heart, taking possession of the Promised Land, as we inherit the good life promised us by God through the transformation of our heart. When we quiet our mind our heart is given a voice, its intuition for perfect timing bringing thoughts to our mind, spontaneously. This is the second phase of the process at work, which is not activated by the power of the mind; not by analysis or rationalization, but through the power of the heart; through intuition and revelation, reaching into the kingdom of God. We can help facilitate the release of our suppressed emotions by quieting our mind, and through body disciplines that aid in the opening of the energy centers of the body.

Weeks 3 & 4
Darkening the sun and the moon

Make note of the spontaneous thoughts that are coming to you in relation to your father and your mother.

As mentioned, the *what? how? why? when?* in the definition of *manna* has to do with the questions we will more than likely find ourselves asking as we experience this part of the process. Through the power of the heart we will be brought into the truth of all that was painful in connection with our father and mother. Through this awareness we validate to ourselves the effects their negative words and actions had upon our heart. Our holy spirit acts as the divine messenger that brings these well-hidden, repressed memories to mind. In expressing these memories by writing them down, the power behind the *spirit* that brought them to our mind, and the power of the written *word*, culminate, which is *christ*. The healing begins, the seed of validated truth penetrating our mind, facilitating the process that will free us of the pain and the anger we have kept bottled up for all these years. When the source of the painful memory is revealed to us, the spiritual light of that truth transforms the painful emotion associated with it, removing the painful, deep-seated memory once and for all as the energy that empowered it is no more, as it is written, *"and there was no more sea"* (Revelation 21:1).

It is of upmost importance that we allow this part of the process to take place naturally, spontaneously, not induced through the fearful and controlling power of the mind, which being inferior, will repress the memories carrying the greatest degree of negative energy, acting as a haven, protecting them. This internal healing process is bound to set off an internal power struggle as the holy spirit of our heart seeks to expose what our mind wants to hide and protect. To keep its power, the mind will speak its lies, trying to convince us that engaging in any process that brings up the negative things from our past, is wrong, counterproductive, or unnecessary. Our mind might tell us the things we are writing down are insignificant. Don't buy it! We can't change what we don't see. And it is our holy spirit that is bringing this truth to our mind in an effort to make us free, while the spirit of our mind, still in the process of being renewed, wants to hide this transformative truth from us, keeping us in in bondage.

Through this stage of the process we begin to understand how our father's and our mother's wrong way of thinking has become our way of thinking. What is in error or misses the mark, sin, carries negative energy, which keeps the substance of the things we hope for in this life from being seen; from becoming a reality. Through the spontaneous workings of our holy spirit we will reflect on the relationship we had with our father and mother, bringing to light the hurt feelings or painful emotions we have kept hidden deep in our heart. It is the painful emotion that caused the false word or belief to be imprinted on our heart in the first place. What is lacking in our life can be attributed to the negative feeling (*spirit*) and false belief (*word*) our father or mother had pertaining to it. Through what is the beginning of a connection with our heart we expose the reason for the anger we have kept bottled up, which reverberates through the fear we keep hidden in the depths of our mind. By allowing the painful truth of our childhood to surface we bring ourselves out of the darkness of repression and into the light of confession, the catalyst for this transformation process, transplanting us from a life of pain and sorrow to a life of joy.

If you have not yet experienced this stage of the process, don't worry. Anxiety is the by-product of a spirit we do not want involved in this process. Keep the desire to see these things alive. Continue with the mental discipline of quieting the mind, and with any physical discipline that calms the body or helps facilitate the release of blocked energies in the body. Relax. Be patient. Don't force the process, but don't allow fear to cause you to run from it either. This is the most important work you will ever do!

"In your patience possess ye your souls." Luke 21:19

More on the Lights of Heaven

The sun symbolizes the spirit or energy of our father and the ego, and the moon, the spirit or energy of our mother and the emotions. The stars also have a double meaning. They symbolize the spirit or energy of our siblings, relatives, or anyone that we closely related to throughout our life, the relationships of which are to be processed in the same manner as we did with our father and mother, allowing the negative aspects of these relationships, and the part we played in that negativity to surface. We should be able to identify some common threads in these relationships with reference to our thoughts, feelings, and behaviors. The stars of heaven also symbolize our birth sign. God makes it perfectly clear that we are not to make a god out of these lights of heaven (Deuteronomy 4:19). We are not to worship or serve them, which is to let them rule our life. We are to use them for their intended purpose— to lead us to the truth about ourselves, as the stars led those that were wise to Jesus. The eleven stars that bowed down to Joseph also symbolize our astrological birth charts, each of us likened to an individual star, influenced by the planets; by our astrological position in the cosmos. By concentrating on the negative traits of our birth sign, and the negative aspects in our chart, we have even more information that will help us transform negative into positive. One more tool we can use to change that which does not serve us in a productive way, resulting in a more joyful life.

Grandfathers and Grandmothers

A good man leaveth an inheritance to his children's children: and the wealth of the sinner is laid up for the just. Proverbs 13:22

God's Word tells us that the inheritance is to be passed down to the grandchildren, the physical revealing the spiritual, as our grandparent's spiritual *inheritance* is passed down to us either directly, or indirectly through our parents. So we can identify certain spiritual traits and beliefs, and behaviors we inherited from our grandparents as well. The *just* are those that judge or overcome these undesirable traits and behaviors. If you find you are unable to move past blame as you are taken through this process, and if it is still possible to do so, try to engage your father or mother in a conversation about their childhood.

Using this approach myself, I found it to be quite helpful. As has been done throughout time, Mom and I shared a bottle of wine, making our hearts merry, to use a biblical phrase, which allows the heart to open up, and communicate her deepest feelings. It is the painful experiences from our past that we have difficulty communicating, the mind doing a great job of repressing these memories as a means of protecting the heart from any further pain. The mind serves as the problem solver, which is now the problem! The mind is hiding and protecting what the heart needs to expose in order to be healed of these painful emotions. That's the good in alcohol, which releases our inhibitions, allowing us to express what we normally would not, bringing down the wall that stands between our mind and heart. And guilt, which is fear-driven, makes it difficult for parents to admit to their short-comings; to validate or take responsibility for the painful effects their actions had upon their children; a parental validation that allows for a quicker release of these painful, negative and destructive, emotions we suppress. I learned a lot about my mom that night, awareness that helped me to move past blame, and into true forgiveness. We can't give what we weren't given. After our conversation I understood why she was unable to satisfy the emotional needs I had as a child. But through God's amazing healing

67

process I became my own mother by proxy, nurturing the wounded child within.

Issachar

Issachar is a strong ass couching down between two burdens: And he saw that rest was good, and the land that it was pleasant; and bowed his shoulder to bear, and became a servant unto tribute. Genesis 49:14.

The word *Issachar* means *he will bring a reward,* the word *reward* going back to the root word meaning, *to hire, to hire out self.* But to understand what has taken place or befallen us from within we need to understand the circumstances surrounding the conception of Issachar.

Overview: In the days of the wheat harvest Reuben goes into the field and finds *mandrakes;* love apples, and brings them to his mother Leah. Rachel wants the mandrakes. Leah says to Rachel, *"It is a small matter that thou hast taken my husband: and wouldest thou take away my son's mandrakes also?"* A husband is anything that has rule over us, positive or negative. Rachel then strikes a deal with Leah, allowing her to lie with Jacob, her husband, in exchange for the mandrakes or love apples. Leah then says to Jacob, *"Thou must come in unto me; for surely I have hired thee with my son's mandrakes."* And thereby was Issachar conceived.

And Leah said, God hath given me my hire, because I have given my maiden to my husband: and she called his name Issachar.

Genesis 30:18

Reuben goes into the field, symbolizing the world, where he finds an aphrodisiac; the love that engulfs us the moment we arrive in this world. But it doesn't take long for *Leah,* symbolizing the *Mind,* to figure out that the mandrakes can be used to get what she wants, as the infant using the love

68

coming in from the world through his parents to get what he wants, satisfying the lustful desires of his mind. *Rachel,* symbolizing the *Heart,* wants and needs love. But it's not love that the infant or child receives when his lustful desires are given into. In the birth order, *Issachar* precedes *Zebulun,* the order in which they are born in us. First we *hire* ourselves to do our own thinking, our wages paid in wrong thoughts, which we then become *inhabited* with. They become habits. The word *Zebulun* means *habitation, reside, dwell with.* Issachar and Zebulun are sons of Leah, symbolizing the Mind, which choosing to accept wrong thoughts has brought about transference of power; from love to lust. The word *mandrakes* goes back to the root word meaning *to boil,* symbolizing the process that transforms lust to love— flesh to spirit.

Issachar is a strong ass...

The word *ass* means *to boil up, to ferment (with scum).* Turning up the heat by being brutally honest with ourselves will expose these destructive thoughts and beliefs, allowing them to boil up, the impurities of the flesh formed by our word of error brought to the surface like the skins of the grapes that rise up in the wine-making process. Once we see them we can skim them off, removing what is worthless while empowering that which is good. The process for making *wine,* symbolizing *spirit,* reveals the process by which we perfect the spirit of love from within our own heart.

couching down between two burdens:

Our burden is our word of error. On one side, we have the burden of knowing we are responsible for what we have manifested in our life. On the other side, we have the burden of doing something about it.

And he saw that rest was good, and the land that it was pleasant;...

The land that is pleasant is the Promised Land, symbolizing the good life promised to us by God. But it is not time to rest. It is time to battle against the unholy inhabitants of our heart, driving them out so we can possess this new land or life, entering a mental and emotional state that allows us to truly and freely enjoy its pleasures.

When he speaketh fair, believe him not: for there are seven abominations in his heart. Proverbs 26:25

These *seven abominations* are represented by the seven nations that inhabited the Promised Land, all of them *Canaanite* tribes, meaning *to humiliate,* revealing the ways in which we humiliate ourselves and others; spiritually and physically. When the two spies were sent into the Promised Land to size up the strength of the enemy, they returned with this report. *"The Lord hath delivered into our hands all the land; for even all the inhabitants of the country do faint because of us"* (Joshua 2:24). The two spies represent the two witnesses— spirit and word, through which we win the battle over these internal enemies, a battle that pits spirit against spirit and word against word; love against fear and truth against lie. The more we engage our holy spirit to bring us into the light of truth, the more we flex the spiritual muscle of our heart, gaining strength as our unholy spirit and word of error gives way to God's holy spirit and word of truth, our internal *"antichrist"* giving way to *christ,* through which we are healed. It's a spiritual battle, referred to as *"the battle of Armageddon"* (Revelation 16:16), through which we take possession of our spiritual inheritance of a joyful life, restoring our true spiritual essence; becoming our true self.

and bowed his shoulder to bear, and became a servant unto tribute.

To bow our shoulder illustrates our willingness to carry our own burden, taking responsibility for the consequences of our own word, which we laid upon ourselves and others.

70

What caused Issachar to become *a servant unto tribute,* the word *tribute* meaning *a tax in the form of forced labor* was choosing rest over doing the spiritual works that make us free of the false beliefs that keep us in bondage.

These first six sons of Jacob are the sons of Leah, spirits born of the lust of the flesh, giving power to our many disorders and compulsions. As we pass through the next four sons of Leah and Rachel's bondmaids we will execute judgment upon our mental and emotional bondages, which are keeping us from being completely free. After the birth of these six sons Leah gives birth to a daughter named *Dinah,* which means *judge,* representing the spiritual judgment revealed through the twelve sons of Jacob.

A Misconception about Judgment

We have been taught by Christian leaders not to judge one another. *"Judge not, that ye be not judged,"* But this fear of being judged if we judge another is the same fear that keeps one from judging themselves, which is absolutely necessary if we want to change our life. The error lies not in our judgment of others, which is the mirror through which we are to judge ourselves. The error lies in our failure to see if we are guilty of the same thing that we are judging another for.

And why beholdest thou the mote that is in thy brother's eye, but perceivest not the beam that is in thine own eye?... cast out first the beam out of thine own eye, and then shalt thou see clearly to pull out the mote that is in thy brother's eye. Luke 6:41,42

In completing our own righteous judgment, overcoming the error or sin that exists in us, we are able to rightly judge the actions of others. Our judgments, made from a holy spirit, will be right judgments. Having gone through the spiritual judgment ourselves, we are more tolerant and understanding;

71

yet do not condone the unrighteous actions of those that have yet to judge themselves.

Week 5
Identifying our inhabitants

Through the power of our holy spirit we will be brought into the light of thoughts that our mind has become inhabited with. Make note of these habitual thoughts, many of which will have been passed down to us through our father, mother, and those that influenced our thinking throughout our life. It is this error in thought, speaking from an error in belief that has us living a life we don't want to live. This less-than-perfect life is based on an image; a projection of what we were taught to believe. We should also look for patterns of thinking and behaving that oppose what we saw growing up. In our disdain for these behaviors we might have rebelled against them, swinging in the opposite direction. We may have had a bad experience with alcohol so we made the decision to never drink, or judge those that do. The problem is not the alcohol, but the pain caused by the behavior of the one addicted to the alcohol. The anger caused by the painful experience dwells in our heart, which determines the way we feel, and subsequently think about alcohol, or any number of things. So once again, we see that through our need to control the external stuff we discover our internal stuff; the fear and the anger, which leads to the need for control, to impose laws that restrict and limit us, which is bondage.

We judge Zebulun and Issachar by becoming aware of the wrong thoughts that we have become inhabited with, and by understanding that we alone are responsible for keeping these false perceptions alive. The color associated with Zebulun and Issachar is yellow.

Chapter Seven
Judging Dan

Dan, his people shall mete-out-judgment, (to all) of Israel's branches together... Genesis 49:16 (The Five Books of Moses)

D an, son by *Rachel's bondmaid,* revealing its association with the *bondage of the Heart.* The word *Dan* means *judge,* and we judge all of these tribes simultaneously as we go through the process of overcoming each false belief of our heart.

Dan shall be a serpent by the way, an adder in the path, that biteth the horse heels, so that his rider shall fall backward. I have waited for thy salvation, O Lord. Genesis 49:17,18

The *horse* symbolizes the *motivation that carries us to destruction,* which this judgment associated with the bondage of the heart, averts. We are the *rider,* being driven by a negative and destructive force. To save ourselves from its dangerous effects we must stop this motivation that will not end well, by taking part in another symbolic passover.

Then sang Moses and the children of Israel this song unto the Lord, and spake, saying, I will sing unto the Lord, for he hath triumphed gloriously: the horse and his rider hath he thrown into the sea. The Lord is my strength and song, and he is become my salvation: he is my God, and I will prepare him an habitation; my father's God, and I will exalt him. Exodus 15:1,2

They sang this song of victory after passing through the Red Sea, the *sea* symbolizing the *hidden negatively-charged thoughts* that inhabit our subconscious mind. This spiritual passover takes place when we pass over from becoming aware of these thoughts to overcoming them, a righteous judgment that prepares *an habitation* for God, *a purified heart* for God's two divine attributes of holy spirit and holy seed; love and truth. In doing this we *exalt* God.

To translate the kingdom from the house of Saul, and to set up the throne of David over Israel and over Judah, from Dan even to Beersheba. 2 Samuel 3:10

We are to translate our internal kingdoms of mind and heart, from king *Saul;* a spirit that *demands*, through the power of our mind, that we obey these destructive thoughts, to king *David;* a spirit that persuades us to overcome them, which is *Love.* The word *Beersheba* means *well of an oath,* the word *oath* meaning *seven (as the sacred full one), seven times, a week,* representing our seven spiritual weeks of spiritual works, completing the righteous judgment that results in a new life.

And I saw another sign in heaven, great and marvelous, seven angels having the seven last plagues; ... And I saw as it were a sea of glass mingled with fire: and them that had gotten victory over the beast, and over his image, and over his mark, and over the number of his name, stand on the sea of glass... And they sang the song of Moses, the servant of God, and the song of the Lamb, saying, Great and marvelous are thy works ... Revelation 15:1-3

The song of Moses, the same song of victory the children of Israel sang after passing through the Red Sea, illustrating our passing through or becoming aware of the thoughts that have been hiding in the darkness of repression. After that, we begin the next phase of the spiritual process, symbolized by the *seven angels,* through which we will experience levels of self-awareness. An *angel* is a *messenger,* seven of Jacob's sons acting as spiritual messengers, bringing messages from the subconscious to the conscious mind, a great and marvelous work taking place in that spiritual *heaven* called *the mind.* The *seven plagues* are fulfilled through our judgment; by overcoming of the negative aspects of these sons or tribes. The *sea of glass mingled with fire* symbolizes God's *judgment,* through which *see through* our negative and destructive beliefs, giving us victory over the *beast* and *his image.* The *mark* of the beast is *destruction,* the consequence of worshiping the beast, which is the false belief, and the message of Jacob's son, Dan.

Jeroboam, the king of Israel, set up image, the gold calf in Dan and Bethel, symbolizing the false religious and self-image, which makes up the beast, which is carrying us down the road to destruction on a soul-level. The gold calf in Dan, which is the outward image we choose to believe, such as religion, will mirror the gold calf in Bethel, which is the inward image; the false personal beliefs formed by painful personal experiences. It seems the more emotional pain we experienced throughout our life; the more likely we are to choose a belief that projects us outside of ourselves, so we never have to go within where all that pain is. But this only serves to strengthen our Jerusalem of bondage, whose wall of false peace keeps us separated from the very thoughts and feelings that keep us bound to our physical and spiritual addictions. Our image may have us seeking an external kingdom, when Jesus tells us expressly that the kingdom of God is within us. We may serve an image that has us focusing all of our attention on what we put into our body, when Jesus tells us explicitly that it is not what enters our body that defiles us, but what proceeds out of our heart. We may serve an image that has us expending our energy trying to save others, instead of entering within and saving our self through that spiritual healing power called *christ.* The *king of Israel* set up these images to keep the people from going into *Jerusalem,* just as the *spirit of the Mind,* fear, sets up images to keep us from entering our *Heart,* the fear of not conforming to these false religious beliefs being the same fear that will keep us from communicating with our heart, where they will discover our false personal beliefs. These are the *"gods made by hand;"* made by an unholy power.

If we were abandoned as a child, we may have formed an image or belief that will make sure that we never put ourselves in a situation where we risk being abandoned again. Motivated by fear, we will never engage in, or fully commit to a relationship. If we lacked nurturing as a child, we may have opted not to have children, fearing we lack the ability to nurture, visiting the same emotional pain we experienced as a child upon our own child. These beliefs will have us betraying the desires of our heart, keeping from us the very things that would bring us our greatest joy. We erect images as a means of compensating for what we lacked as children. If we lacked stability in our childhood, we may have given life to an image that provides us with that stability, no matter how far removed from reality it might be. If our childhood pain was associated with money matters, we may have become obsessed with acquiring money, never having to experience the pain associated with money again. We will cause ourselves a great deal of stress trying to live up to these images, and at the expense of all that really matters, connecting with self. We set up these images as a means of subduing the unholy spirit of our mind, fear, not aware of the paradox: the image perpetuates the fear, which sustains these pressing thoughts.

It is the painful emotions associated with our past that give power to these thoughts that continually impact our mind, as the moon gives power to sea's perpetual tides. Every major decision we make will have to be sanctioned by the false image we have given power to. These beliefs limit us, keeping us from doing the things that would bring to us the desires of our heart, bringing us our greatest joy.

When we experience emotional trauma we are filled with fear, the unholy spirit or negative energy of the lie we tell ourselves in that particular moment in time. And we opted for this lie for one of two reasons. We are taught from infancy that we have control over our external world. When our world hits us with something we cannot control, fear takes over our mind, giving power to the lie. We will blame ourselves for the painful things we are experiencing, taking on the guilt for things that we have no control over, even shutting off our emotions altogether as a means of protecting ourselves from the pain. The other reason for accepting the lie is we fear the truth will only add more pain. Either way, this lie becomes our word, which becomes our burden, which we will carry as emotional pain until we are delivered of it through the birth of truth.

By allowing our holy spirit to move us back in time, to the moment of trauma, we connect with the painful emotions that sustain the false belief. Anger is the primary emotion of the heart, and we are angry because of the wrong or evil, the error or sin, we suffered, directly or indirectly. When we relinquish the blame and guilt we have carried for the things we couldn't control, we give ourselves permission to connect with the hidden feelings of our heart. This emotional release is the shaking of the earth; shaking the foundation. By replacing the lie we told ourselves during the trauma with truth we tear down the false image or belief, and subsequent wrong thought, absolving the negative energies of fear, anger, and control; the unholy spirits of Reuben, Simeon, and Levi.

It is at Dan that we execute judgment upon all the tribes, overcoming the negative aspects attributed to them. We overcome the fear of our mind and the anger of our heart through awareness, which is the light needed to transform these negative and destructive energies. We overcome the control behind our unhealthy behaviors through the action of our body. We put the negative energy behind the destructive habitual behavior in remission by doing the opposite of what our mind, being led by the destructive belief of our heart, is driving us to do. This is repentance, which is a reversal of another's decision. Through this judgment or action we reverse the decision of the false image or belief, which is out to destroy our body. The body follows the mind, but we need to reverse that, and use our body to override our mind, stopping the destructive action. If you are thinking you tried this already, and it didn't work, it's because the power through which you tried to control the destructive behavior was self-will; the lower power of the mind, a control driven by fear; the fear of relapsing into the addiction, for example. Using self-control to control the addiction does not work! *"How can Satan cast out Satan?"* (Mark 3:23). Success will come by using divine will; the higher power of the heart. Calling upon this higher power, according to God's 12-step process, is revitalizing it through the discipline of quieting the mind; *"silence in heaven"* (Revelation 8:1), which takes power from the mind, putting the fear in remission, the body, led by divine will, overriding the destructive goading spirit of the mind.

Dan shall be a snake by the wayside, a horned-viper on the path who bites the horse's heels so that his rider tumbles backward.

(The Five Books of Moses)

Dan means *judge.* The *snake* symbolizes our *iniquity or wrong thought.* The *horse* symbolizes our *wrong motivation,* which is driven by the false belief, carrying us down the road to spiritual and physical destruction. The snake has the power to stop our destructive motivation because the habitual destructive thoughts of our mind are a reflection of the destructive beliefs of our heart, which we have the power to judge or overcome through *christ*— the healing anointing of spirit and truth, the light of truth destroying the destroyer. It will be our love of truth that brings the *spirit of truth* that reveals the *Wicked* one within us, saving us from ourselves.

78

For the mystery of iniquity doth already work: only he who now letteth will let, until he (Satan) *be taken out of the way. And then shall the Wicked be revealed, whom the Lord shall consume with the spirit of his mouth and shall destroy with the brightness of his coming: Even him, whose coming is after the working of Satan with all power and signs and lying wonders, And with all deceivableness of unrighteousness in them that perish; because they received not the love of the truth, that they might be saved. 2 Thessalonians 2:7-10*

The *spirit of his mouth* is the *spirit of truth* (John 16:13), the *brightness of his coming*, the *light of truth,* which the holy spirit of our heart delivers, saving us from the primordial lying thoughts and painful emotions that gave power to our false beliefs, which perpetuate our destructive thoughts, the signs of which are seen in our destructive actions or behaviors.

Why do ye not understand my speech? even because ye cannot hear my word. Ye are of your father the devil, and the lusts of your father ye will do. He was a murderer from the beginning, and abode not in the truth, because there was no truth in him. When he speaketh a lie, he speaketh of his own: for he is a liar, and the father of it. John 8:43,44

We do not hear the truth because we give reverence to another *father;* a father that sows lies through fear. It is this destructive energy that generates the lust that makes us want, and choose, what isn't good for us. The lies of our mind murder the truth of our heart; crucifying it daily through our believing this word of error, which we demonstrate through actions that stand in support it, as Adam and Eve obeyed the word of the serpent. *"Two nations are in thy womb"* (Genesis 25:23), two opposing forces are in our heart; true image and false image. The words of the true image are compassionate and kind. The words of the false image are critical, self-loathing, condemning. Judging the negative and destructive thoughts by opposing them through action takes power from the false image or belief, the anger of which has been empowering our self-hatred, which we take out on our body. These false images carry the energy that leads us down the road to destruction through our many disorders, phobias, addictions, and compulsions. Divine truth overturns the false images set up on *"the fleshy tables of the heart"* (2 Corinthians 3:3). When we make the transition from awareness of these negative thoughts to action against them, we are experiencing our second *passover.* Our first passover is from knowledge to understanding. Our second passover is from understanding to wisdom— action.

And the Jews' Passover was at hand, and Jesus went up to Jerusalem, And found there in the temple those that sold oxen and sheep and doves, and the changers of money sitting: And when he had made a scourge of small cords, he drove them all out of the temple, and the sheep, and the oxen; and poured out the changers' money, and overthrew the tables; And said unto them that sold doves, Take these things hence; make not my Father's house an house of merchandise. John 2:13-16

Whatever our addiction, the consequence of our false image or belief, it can be overcome with truth. If the belief has become so immense or intense that it has distorted our mind to the point that we are not able to see it, we will need help getting through the thick veil or wall of iniquity that obscures it. We may not be able to identify our false image, to know when it is speaking to us, but we still have our feelings, which will let us know deep from within that something is wrong. And if our heart should fail us, we have our body, whose actions and condition cannot, and should not, be denied. And if our external witness is not enough, we must go out even further. By asking for the truth from those who love us we help facilitate the destruction of the dangerous belief that has led to our disorder, addiction, disease, or compulsion. And if we are chosen to be the dispensers of this truth we have a spiritual and moral obligation to give it out. The one asking for truth will be fighting the fear of asking, and the anger that may rise up in him when he receives it. We should expect to do no less. You may have to fight the fear of telling them what they need to hear, knowing that they may hate you for giving them the truth, as it is written, *"ye shall be hated of all men for my name's sake" — for truth's sake.* But far better to be hated for giving them the truth than to be loved for helping to perpetuate the lie, whereby one hides his light under a bushel (Matthew 5:15).

I have waited for thy salvation, O Lord. Genesis 49:18

I wait-in-hope for your deliverance O YHWH

(The Five Books of Moses).

Salvation is of the soul, the vital principle in man credited to the faculty of thought, emotion, and action. Our *salvation* or *deliverance* is from our negative thoughts and painful emotions, which drive our destructive actions. We *wait-in hope* by doing the works of salvation, which saves us from our self. Hope is faith, but faith without works is dead, having no power to deliver us.

When we quiet our mind we pass power over to our heart; a spiritual passover that gives power to the two witnesses of the heart. The holy spirit of our heart can now influence the thoughts of our mind. With the unholy spirit of our mind broken through the discipline of silence, we give power to the word of truth of our heart, which is now penetrating our mind. We are to use this truth to fight against the negative influences that are fighting to take possession of our mind. Awareness of our perpetual destructive thoughts is the light that begins the transformation process. Coming into the truth of what is at the root of our destructive thoughts and behaviors is the greater degree of light that takes power away from our self-will and hands it over to divine will; the control exhibited through the power of our mind giving way to the divine will working through our mind by way of the divine power of our heart. If we do not transform the destructive energy responsible for the disorder, addiction, disease, or compulsion through the higher power of our heart, the destructive energy will remain, being transferred, finding another outlet, maybe one that is not so obvious. The only power that can make us permanently free of our spiritual and physical bondages or addictions is the power of truth, which flows forth from the heart through the power of love. Love and truth, the two things needed for the creation of a new heaven and a new earth— a new mind and a new heart!

Dan was the son of *Rachel's bondmaid,* symbolizing the *Heart's bondage* to false beliefs, which we are to judge, overcoming the painful emotions that empower the fearful thoughts that drive our destructive behaviors, ending the vicious cycle!

We judge Dan by overcoming our false religious and personal images or beliefs through the power of our heart, through which we are healed. The color associated with Dan is green.

Chapter Eight
Judging Gad

Gad, a troop shall overcome him: but he shall overcome at the last.

Gad, goading robber-band will goad him, yet he will goad at their heel.

Genesis 49:19 (The Five Books of Moses)

Gad, son by *Leah's bondmaid*, revealing its association with the *bondage of the Mind*, and the body. The word *Gad* means *to crowd upon, i.e attack:-invade, overcome, to gash (as if by pressing into), gather (selves together, set in troops), cut selves—* describing a spirit that enlists the action of the body through the *goading* of the mind. Goad: that which prods or urges; a stimulus or irritating incentive; an impetus: an impelling force or impulse, describing this destructive energy that influences the mind, urging the body to perform the destructive act, robbing us of our freedom by keeping us bound to the addiction. Gad is a very oppressive spirit, a tyrannical energy that causes mental and physical anguish. It is the nasty spirit responsible for the cruel and destructive addiction called *cutting*, found in the definition of *Gad*. Having suffered with anorexia in former years I am very familiar with this destructive spirit. In the end, I could barely bring myself to eat, my 5'7" body going from 125 to 95 pounds. The good news is, we have the power to overcome this unhealthy spirit.

Gad, son of *Leah's bondmaid*, symbolizing the *Mind's bondage* to fearful and untruthful thoughts, the fruit of which is this goading spirit, all working together to limit us, keep us in bondage or addiction. The connection taking place between our mind and heart through this process allows us to feel the restriction caused by this energy; an unholy spirit that goads us to act out the destructive behavior through the relentless and impulsive thought. It is also the spirit that causes us to isolate ourselves, or makes us feel as if we are all alone in this world, or to feel confined or closed in— claustrophobic.

Gad, a troop shall overcome him...   (King James Bible)
Gad, goading robber-band will goad him... (The Five Books of Moses)

The *troop* or *band* that robs the mind and body of its freedom are the negative and destructive conscious thoughts of our mind, which are being generated by the well-hidden energy and belief of the subconscious mind; the unholy spirit and word dwelling in the heart, which the holy spirit of the heart is attempting to communicate to the mind, but which man continues to resist it (Acts 7:51). The mind and heart must be reconciled. This will require us to quiet our mind, through which the power of the ego, the personality component that most immediately controls behavior, recedes. The *"seventh seal"* or chakra, which opens as a result of this silence (Revelation 8:1), activates the higher power or holy spirit of our heart. This positive energy brings the light of truth to our mind, exposing what has been hidden in our heart. It is this spiritual light that helps transform the negative energy bound up in the heart, charging the mind and body with positive energy, helping us to overcome this *goading spirit.*

Through eastern energy work or disciplines that facilitate the release of blocked energy in the six chakras of the body, we aid in the release of our suppressed emotions. Through God's 12-step process, the self-will or control of the mind gives way to a divine will or control of the heart called temperance, the fruit of our holy spirit, allowing us the freedom to enjoy the pleasures of this life without the burden of addiction, or fear of relapsing into addiction. The primary emotion or unholy spirit of the heart is anger, the heart's natural response to the false image or belief that has been set up in that spiritual temple called the heart. Jesus revealed this spiritual truth to us when he got angry after seeing the images that were set up in the physical temple, the carnal revealing the spiritual. The spirit that works in conjunction with this unholy anger is self-will. Anger and control; *"Simeon and Levi are brethren; instruments of cruelty,"* the two-fold power that drives our cruel and destructive habitual behaviors. We can however use this anger for the good by doing what Jesus did, directing it toward the false image or belief, even if we don't know what it is yet. We can also use our self-will for the good, using self-control to stop the destructive behavior *until* we have done enough internal work to put the energy driving the addiction into remission, as we continue to be immersed in truth, overcoming or overturning the false image or belief, through which the lower power of our mind gives way to the higher power of our heart, excess giving way to moderation.

but he shall overcome at the last. (King James Bible)

yet he will goad at their heel. (The Five Books of Moses)

For some this *goading spirit* has intensified to such a degree that they are unable to function with ease in everyday life. Our phobias are holding us in a virtual prison. We are afraid to enter into an elevator, fly in an airplane, drive over a bridge, leave our house, and the list goes on. At the root of these phobias is our spiritual addiction to fear, which if allowed to rule the mind for a prolonged time effects the actions of our body. Our desire to set ourselves free of this prison is love, the positive emotion that is one with our holy spirit, which charges the body with positive energy, giving us the power to oppose the mind, by-passing its debilitating fear. What we will discover by using the action of our body to fight against the destructive and limiting thoughts of our mind is that these thoughts were lies. It is this degree of truth that gives us the power or strength to do the things we once feared to do.

For the flesh desires the contrary of the spirit, and the spirit the contrary to the flesh; for these are opposed to each other; so that you do not perform the things that you wish.   Galatians 5:17

It is not our physical flesh body that is contrary to our holy spirit. It is our spiritual flesh, formed by our word of error; by the false beliefs that speak through the lies of our mind, the spirit of which is fear, which are opposed to God's spirit and word; love and truth. By teaming the action of our body with the loving and compassionate spirit that we empower through a sincere desire to change our life for the better, we take our mind out from the fear that feeds the destructive control, which has caused us to make some really bad choices throughout our life. If we take a good look at our life we will discover many ways in which we limit ourselves on a physical level, which is really a mental limitation brought on by fear. We may be afraid to commit to a marriage, or have children. There is no denying that these are a matter of choice, but we need to look beneath that choice and see if we can identify any false image or belief that may be lurking there. We accepted these lies in our heart through the power of the painful emotions attached to our painful experiences. For example, a young girl watches as her mother gives birth. The infant is still-born, the traumatic experience forming the perception in the young girl's mind that giving birth will have devastating results. The mental energy that gave power to this false perception or lie is fear. The emotional energy tied to the traumatic experience causes the false perception to become a false belief. The truth is, most births do not end in sorrow, but in joy, classifying this belief as false. The young girl, now a woman, may be able to intellectualize this truth, believe it at the mind level. But until she believes it at the heart level through the conception of truth at a heart level, which transforms the emotions associated with the traumatic experience, she will continue to fear childbirth.

The painful events that took place in our life established these fears and misconceptions, many of which keep us from actualizing our true desires. But we can fight against these fear-driven lies by using the action of our body to discredit them. Using the action of the body to overcome the fear of the mind is one thing. But using the power of our mind alone to try to overcome the addiction is quite another. Self-control, which many are mistaking for their higher power, is just what it says it is; a control imposed on one's self through one's own mind. This lower power, while giving us the ability to refrain from the habit or addiction, as the body follows the mind, is also responsible for the relapse because this lower power is rendered powerless in times of emotional crisis. The self-willed control of abstinence, while serving to keep the body alive, is still a law, one many will remain under for the rest of their lives because they fear the relapse, or the process that will take them on a journey through their heart, where they will discover the root cause of their addiction. Fear becomes the internal law that serves to keep the body in restraint, but it also serves to sustain the root of excess that remains in the heart. Abstinence, the denial of the appetites, may stop the external addiction, but it does nothing to stop the internal addiction. The energy that drives the external addiction still exists, transferred to yet another addiction, as energy is either transformed or transferred. Now one is under both the law of restraint, and the law of excess.

... for ye make clean the outside of the cup and of the platter, but within they are full of extortion and excess... cleanse first that which is within the cup and platter, that the outside of them may be clean also."
Matthew 23:25,26

If our thoughts and emotions are pure, our actions will be pure, finding a perfect healthy balance.

We judge Gad by becoming aware of the unholy spirit that controls our body through the fear-driven lies of our mind, and by enlisting our body to overcome this impetus goading spirit by doing the opposite of what it is driving us to do. The color associated with Gad is blue.

Chapter Nine
Judging Asher

Out of Asher his bread shall be fat, and he shall yield royal dainties. Genesis 49:20

Asher, his nourishment is rich, he gives forth king's dainties.
(The Five Books of Moses)

Asher, son by *Leah's bondmaid,* revealing its association with the *bondage of the Mind,* and the body. The word *Asher* means *happy,* providing a much different feeling than that of God. The word *bread* means *to battle, consume, overcome.* As we continue to battle the bondages of our mind and body, phobias and compulsions, overcoming the negative influences of our mind through the action of our body, we must also continue to strengthen the positive influence of our heart. In quieting our mind we give power to the holy spirit of our heart, which it uses to influence the thoughts of our mind, giving us the strength we need in moments of weakness, or in times of emotional crisis, the strength to push through the contractions of temptation or tribulation. With our body working in conjunction with the higher power of our heart, we expose the lies of our mind, removing their power, the wellspring of fear. The success of overcoming the limitations brought on by the fear of our mind will have us experiencing the positive aspect of *Asher; happiness* that comes with feeling some degree of physical freedom. We will finally be able to exhale!

The word *dainties* means *a delicacy, or (abstr.) pleasure, delight, to be soft or pleasant.* Overcoming through our higher power is going to make us softer, more pleasant human beings. No longer acting as our own internal tyrant, issuing forth unrealistic commands through thoughts that demand, through the fear of our mind, that we do this or that, we become a much happier and healthier person. By engaging our holy spirit, whose positive energy overrides the negative influences of our mind, we bring forth the fruits of the spirit; kindness and compassion, releasing us from the works of the flesh; cruel and unmerciful acts we imposed upon ourselves because of this invisible flesh formed by false perceptions and beliefs, giving power to the unholy spirits are fear, anger, control, and impatience. Every time we battle against the destructive influences of our mind through the action of our body we give *nourishment* to the holy spirit of our heart. This spiritual battle is the true meaning of a holy war, through which the spiritual kingdoms of our mind and heart are taken out from under the rule of an oppressive demanding spirit and handed over to a kind and compassionate loving spirit.

The negative aspect of *Asher* is *happiness* derived from delusion. We keep ourselves deluded by keeping our mind separated from our heart, symbolized by the veil that stood between the worldly sanctuary and the holiest place of all (Hebrews 9:1-3). The result of this separation is false peace. Some obtain this false peace or happiness by choosing a belief that keeps them separated from their feelings, some by blaming others, and some by placing the burden of their destructive behavior upon those closest to them instead of understanding the reason for their bad behavior, and then doing something about it. The other person is put in the position of carrying the weight, burdened not only by their bad behavior, but by the emotional pain that comes with experiencing their negative and destructive behavior, time and again.

For every man shall bear his own burden. Galatians 6:5

The burdener is happy. He has found someone else to carry his cross, placing his burden of sin upon a human scapegoat. Or so he thinks!

And as for the prophet, and the priest, and the people, that shall say, The burden of the Lord. I will even punish that man and his house... And the burden of the Lord shall ye mention no more: for every man's word shall be his burden; for ye have perverted the words of the living, God, of the Lord of host our God. Jeremiah 23:34,36

Gad and Asher, born of Leah's bondmaid Zilpah symbolize the two evil spirits or negative energies that take us from the depths of depression to the heights of elation, and back again. We call the person in whom this spiritual action takes place frequently, and with intensity, bi-polar, an outward sign of an inward imbalance, which will correct itself through continued application of God's 12-step healing process. It's been said that depression is anger turned inward. Depression sets in when the reality of our life fails to agree with what we had envisioned for our life. Anger, the unholy spirit of the false belief, which has us living a life we don't want to be living, is the source of our depression.

Then there are those individuals that walk around with a smile on their face at all times, hiding behind a happy façade. They pretend all is well, covering the pain, never exposing how they truly feel. This is Asher in the negative sense, a spirit many Christians appear to be possessed with. Here the body is working in conjunction with the pretense of the mind. They put on this false front because they believe that to appear as anything other than deliriously happy would reveal to the world that God is not with them. Rather than admit they are unhappy and do something about it, they keep up the pretense, supporting the false image they're projecting.

God hates a lie above all. If we are lying to ourselves by denying how we truly feel, God is not present as God dwells in truth. Being under this delusion is very detrimental to the soul because it prevents us from performing the spiritual works that will bring us true happiness. It also prevents us from getting the much needed help and support we would get if we were reflecting on the outside how we were truly feeling on the inside. And if we have to keep telling ourselves how happy we are we might want to get in touch with the hidden emotions of our heart, as the mind is relentless when it comes to deceiving us as to the true condition of our heart.

...and with every deception of iniquity to those who are perishing, because they admitted not the love of the truth in order that they might be saved. And on this account God sends them an energy of delusion, to their believing the falsehood; in order that all those may be judged who believed not the truth, but approved the iniquity. 2 Thessalonians 2:10-12
(Greek Diaglott)

When we pretend all is well, we are choosing deception, giving power to the *energy of delusion,* rejecting our own salvation. This pretense of the mind only serves to prolong the judgment that heals the soul. Our holy spirit, which moves us into the light of truth, is activated in part by our decision to stop running in circles and change our life. Our tribulation or *time of trouble* also serves to activate our holy spirit, causing us to become introspective, to question our condition or situation, bringing on the contractions that deliver us from our old way of life.

...and there shall be a time of trouble such as never was.. and at that time thy people shall be delivered... Daniel 12:1

Physical infirmity, a form of tribulation, is a blessing if it gets us to cry out to God, activating our higher power. This time of trouble is the travailing, assisting in our spiritual birthing process.

Before she travailed, she brought forth; before her pain came, she was delivered of a man child. Who hath heard such a thing? Who hath seen such things? Shall the earth be made to bring forth in one day? Or shall a nation be born at once? Isaiah 66:7,8

Spiritual birth does not take place in *one day*, or in twenty eight days. It takes time for the heart to conceive and bring forth truth. Isaiah is referring to Christians who claim to be born again before experiencing the emotional pain inherent in the birthing process. They have given birth through the delusion of their mind instead of through the transformation of their heart, a deception of iniquity that bears the negative aspect of Asher— a phony happiness. Giving birth to truth through the power of our holy spirit is hard labor. But like the experience of physical birth, the pain of this spiritual birth is temporary, the joy we receive in the end, eternal. What we are delivered from are the false perceptions and beliefs that would have us living in mental and physical anguish, and in emotional pain for the rest of our lives. But if we experience this birth as God intended, through the reality of our heart, not through the deception of our mind, we will enter that state of complete joy and happiness that comes with being made whole and free; entering the new spiritual Jerusalem.

For it is written that Abraham had two sons, the one by a bondmaid, the other by a freewoman... For this Agar is mount Sinai in Arabia, and answereth to Jerusalem which now is, and is in bondage with her children. But Jerusalem which is above is free... Galatians 4:22,25

The word *Jerusalem* means *founded peaceful*. There are two types of peace; one of the mind, the other of the heart. Peace generated through the power of the mind is false peace. Peace generated through the power of the heart is true peace. Mind peace acts as a wall (Ezekiel 13:9,10), separating us from our heart, protecting our word of error, the source of our bondage. It is this false word that forms the invisible flesh that keeps us in physical and spiritual bondage. And let us not be deceived, we cannot release ourselves from the bondage of our destructive word, or obtain true happiness by thinking positive thoughts, as we shall see in the last of the sons of the bondmaids.

We judge Asher by becoming aware of the unholy spirit that provides us with a false sense of happiness or peace, a deceptive peace founded in part upon a false belief; a religious belief that teaches that we are born in an instant, saved through someone else's labor. The color associated with Asher is purplish blue; indigo.

Chapter Ten
Judging Naphtali

Naphtali is a hind let loose: he giveth goodly words. Genesis 49:21

Naphtali, son by *Rachel's bondmaid*, revealing its association with the *bondage of the Heart*, the last son of the bondmaids of Leah and Rachel pointing to an emotional, rather than a mental or physical, bondage. Using our physical body to oppose the negative and destructive thoughts of our mind has brought us success, and that success is going to make us feel quite happy. But we don't want to stop there. To stop there is to remain under the law, having to work continually to control our mind and body; a never-ending recovery, stamping us with a label that marks us weak and sinful for life. It is God's will that we go beyond the mind-body discipline of stopping our destructive actions through the power of our mind, and into perfection through a heart-discipline, through which the false beliefs and the painful emotions associated with them, are transformed through the light of truth through the power of the heart. We will accomplish this by completing the process, taking the final steps in God's 12-step purification or salvation process; by climbing all twelve rungs of Jacob's ladder, completing our spiritual ascension. The word *Naphtali* means *my wrestling, to twine, to struggle, to wrestle.*

And there Jacob was left alone; and there wrestled a man with him until the breaking of day. Genesis 32:24

The man Jacob wrestled with was himself. Each of us has conceived of good and evil seed, two manner of fruit; the duality of two beliefs, having two very different energies; bi-polar. These two opposing forces; Cain and Abel, Esau and Jacob, creates an internal struggle that ultimately pushes us to come face to face with ourselves— to know ourselves.

...and Rebekah his wife conceived. And the children struggled together within her; and she said, If it be so, why am I thus: And she went to enquire of the Lord. And the Lord said unto her, Two nations are in thy womb, and two manner of people shall be separated from thy bowels... Genesis 27:21-23

The *bowels* symbolize the *heart,* the spiritual womb, where a struggle takes place between two opposing beliefs; the false image and the true image, *two manner of people,* part of us choosing bondage, while the other part of us seeks to be free. The struggle caused by this duality will continue until we are delivered of the falsehood by coming into the light of it, as Jacob wrestled *until the breaking of day.* We come into the light by first being delivered of Esau, the spirit that causes us to forfeit our birthright for *red pottage;* because of a *dangerous arrogance* (Genesis 25:30). This ego-driven spirit of the mind keeps us from humbling ourselves to the process that delivers us from the unrighteous word, delivering us of Esau; from the false religious and personal beliefs that prevent us from giving birth to our true selves, as Jacob was delivered of or separated from Esau after wrestling with the man.

My bowels, my bowels, I am pained at my very heart; my heart maketh a noise in me; I cannot hold my peace, because thou hast heard, O my soul, the sound of the trumpet, the alarm of war. Jeremiah 4:19

When we stop resisting our holy spirit we will hear its voice, the *noise* of those painful emotions that give power to our destructive word. Once we hear our heart, becoming aware

96

of its true condition, we will no longer be able to hold on to the false peace of our mind, which has separated us from our heart. We will have opened the doors to our heart, reaching into the depths of our soul, where the *trumpet* has sounded, declaring war between the false image and the true image.

and I beheld the earth, and, lo, it was without form, and void; and the heavens, and they had no light. Jeremiah 4:23

The *earth* symbolizes the *heart,* which is made *void* in the negative sense when the good seed is rendered ineffective by the evil seed. There is no light because the good seed or word of truth is the light. The earth is made *void* in the positive sense when all the evil seeds or false beliefs are removed. It is in this void that the heart can conceive of the good seed or the light of truth, replacing the darkness formed by our false perceptions and beliefs. Our first heaven and earth passes away through the death of our false perceptions and beliefs; our first creation giving way to a new creation— to a new heaven and a new earth, symbolizing a new mind and a new heart (Revelation 21:1).

Naphtali is a hind let loose …

The word *hind* means *a doe or female deer, strength (in the sense of a ram), anything strong,* symbolizing *the strength of the false belief,* the root cause of disorders, addictions, compulsions, and disease. We must be willing to sacrifice this false word, as Abraham was willing to sacrifice *Isaac,* the negative aspect of which is *mockery*— an imitation, a sham, false. And what was consumed through Abraham's sacrifice was the *ram,* meaning *idolatry;* the worshipping of images.

And Abraham lifted up his eyes, and looked, and behold behind him a ram caught in the thicket by his horns: and Abraham went and took the ram, and offered him up for a burnt offering in the stead of his son.

Genesis 22:13

A *burnt offering* is what we offer up to be *utterly consumed*, which is the *ram,* the worshipping of false images or beliefs. This takes place when they no longer rule our life; when they are dead to us. When we discover and sacrifice them we restore the son of Abraham, restoring the positive aspect of *Isaac,* which is the *promise* or good seed; truth.

God's Ultimate Sacrifice

God sowed His spiritual seed into the mother two thousand years ago in the era of Isaac— *"In Isaac shall thy seed be called"* (Romans 9:7). *"Now the parable is this: the seed is the word of God"* (Luke 8:11). God's word came to take them out from the bondage of the law, as truth comes to take us out from the bondage of unholy spirits and false beliefs. Removing the false word of the heart by way of truth allows us to transcend the law of self will, and experience the liberating effects of divine will. The truth makes us free!

As we enter the third and final era of Jacob we are given one last opportunity in this earth school to make atonement for the death of truth that has taken place within our heart. We do this by taking responsibility for the negative and destructive things we have brought to our life due to our word of error. We continue to empower this destructive word through the unholy destructive spirit of the heart; through the anger that is still hidden deep within us, which is consumed through the higher power of our holy spirit and righteous word; love and truth.

.... He giveth goodly words.

The *goodly words* of Naphtali, a son of Rachel's bondmaid, represent the words that have brought us into bondage; into addiction. These words, which we took for good, believing they were right, have been written upon the tablets

98

of our heart through the power of emotion, in the book that is our life. Our mind has been protecting these evil seeds by suppressing the painful emotions that sustain them, providing the deluded state in which they are given time and space to grow. But the *goodly words* of Naphtali is also pointing us to something pertaining to the *last days;* to a popular belief of today, which teaches that we can change our life, and our world, by thinking positive thoughts. Prayers, affirmations, mantras, and the like will no longer be enough to hold back the flood of evilness quickly rising upon the earth, issuing forth from the destructive energy that still remains in the heart of mankind. Speaking positive words does not transform the heart! To eliminate the wave of destruction we must eliminate the source— the *"lower waters"* or *"sea,"* symbolizing the *negative thoughts* hidden in the depths of our mind. We are instructed through God's creation process to gather them together through the power of our holy spirit so we can see what lies beneath them, in our heart, which speaks to us through a spontaneous remembrance of the negative and painful things we saw, heard, felt, and experienced. Emotional change takes place through the light of awareness, not through the darkness of denial. Avoiding or repressing these thoughts or memories is like putting bandages over *putrifying sores,* hiding their destructive source.

From the sole of the foot even unto the head there is no soundness in it; but wounds, and bruises, and putrifying sores: they have not been closed, neither bound up, neither mollified with ointment. Isaiah 1:6.

The word *mollify* means *to allay the anger of; to placate, to calm.* The word *allay* means *to lessen or relieve (pain or grief); to reduce the intensity of.* We cannot reduce the negative energy bottled up in us by thinking good thoughts. The anger, pain, and grief that still exists in our heart is real, and will only be realized when we stop resisting our holy spirit, allowing it to move these memories and feelings into our awareness so the transformation process can begin. We will not heal the sickness of our heart by taking a positive thinking placebo. We will heal the sickness of our heart with a spiritual ointment; with *christ,* that spiritual anointing that is the *spirit* and *word* of God. The spirit of God is *love* and the word of God is *truth,* working together to purify our emotions, which in turn purify our thoughts, and subsequently our actions, which is purification of the soul— salvation of the soul!

But in the days of the voice of the seventh angel, when he shall begin to sound, the mystery of God should be finished, as he hath declared unto his servants the prophets. Revelation 10:7

The voice of the *seventh angel* sounds when our *holy spirit* begins to bring messages from our heart to our mind. The *mystery of God* pertains to the *kingdom of God* or *realm of the Heart* (Mark 4:11). We enter the realm of our Heart through the power of our holy spirit, where we discover the source of our problems, the mystery of the kingdom of God, solved.

And the voice which I heard from heaven spake to me again, and said, Go and take the little book which is open in the hand of the angel which standeth upon the sea and upon the earth. Revelation 10:8

The *voice* of the spirit speaks to us *from heaven;* from our mind, when the *seventh seal* is opened through *silence in heaven.* We will have to shut off the noise of our mind to connect with the voice of our heart. The *little book,* open in the hand of the seventh angel, is *our life,* opened up to us through the power of our holy spirit, the angel or messenger, which *standeth upon the sea and upon the earth,* symbolizing the connection between *the thoughts of our mind and the feelings of our heart,* the holy spirit of our heart bringing messages from our heart to our mind, and from our mind to our heart, ascending and descending (Genesis 28:12).

100

When our heaven or mind is silent, the holy spirit of our heart is given power, which it uses to move upon the *sea;* upon the negatively charged thoughts and memories hidden in the depths of our mind, moving them up into our conscious mind so we can see lies beneath them in the *earth;* in our heart. Our first heaven and earth, formed through a darkness we mistook for light; an evil we mistook for good, has brought us grief, forming an existence from which we may now want to escape, which is made possible through the creation of a new heaven and earth, formed through the light of truth by way of a holy spirit, through which we enter a new existence; a new state called new Jerusalem.

And I went unto the angel, and said unto him, Give me the little book...
And I took the little book out of the angel's hand, and ate it up; and it
was in my mouth sweet as honey: and as soon as I had eaten it, my belly
was bitter. Revelation. 10:9,10

We need only ask from our heart to have our life opened to us through *the power of the holy spirit,* as it was open in *the hand of the seventh angel.* We took power away from the holy spirit of our heart when our mind began communicating with the unholy spirit of fear, giving power to the lie. In the beginning it was *sweet,* having no immediate unpleasant consequence. But when we accepted the lie into that *belly* called the *heart* through the power of emotion, it became a belief that we would, in time, begin to act upon. These erroneous beliefs are the cause of every wrong and impatient decision we would make throughout our life, the negative, destructive, or unpleasant consequences of which can make us very *bitter.* And the realization that we alone are responsible for the undesirable condition of our life only adds to this bitterness.

...know therefore and see that it is an evil thing, and bitter, that thou has
forsaken the Lord thy God... Jeremiah 2:19

101

We have allowed fear to rule in the place of love, and lies to rule in the place of truth, having *forsaken the Lord*. The gall Jesus was given to drink as he was forsaken on the cross symbolizes the bitterness that results from our forsaking the truth. The painful emotions associated with the false beliefs that have crucified the truth within us contain the evil or negative and destructive energy at the root of diabetes, caused by too much sugar in the blood, the sugar symbolizing the sweetness of a deceptive truth. From the Greek word *diabetes*— *a crossing over or passing through*. As Jacob made a transition by crossing over or through the river Jabbok, we make a transition at Naphtali; from understanding the bondage of our mind and body, to understanding the bondage of our heart, crossing over from knowing we have false beliefs to understanding what they are. It is our passing over from the *"worldly sanctuary,"* symbolizing the *mind*, to the *"holiest place of all,"* symbolizing the heart, the veil between them symbolizing the false peace, which not only prevents us from entering in and connecting with our feelings, but prevents a new and constructive truth from penetrating our heart. It is the light of this new truth that heals us by transforming our negative emotions into positive ones. Believing we can bring calm to our heart, or peace to our earth by thinking good thoughts only serves to shore up this wall of false peace, which stands in the way of us entering into our heart and establishing peace there (Psalms 122).

...and no man was able to enter into the temple, till the seven plagues of the seven angels were fulfilled. Revelation 15:8.

The *temple* symbolizes the *heart*. The *seventh plague* is *hail* (Revelation 16:21), which brings down the wall of false peace that keeps us from entering our heart (Ezekiel (13:13,14). Once we enter that spiritual temple called the heart we are to make sacrifice; sacrificing the false images or beliefs we find there.

Establishing truth in the heart brings true peace. Peace will not come to our earth by changing our thoughts. Peace will come to our earth through the transformation of our hearts.

The land of Zabulon, and the land of Nephtalim, by the way of the sea, beyond Jordan, Galilee of the Gentiles. The people which sat in darkness saw great light; and to them which sat in the region and shadow of death light is sprung up. From that time Jesus began to preach, and to say, Repent: for the kingdom of heaven is at hand. Matthew 4:15-17

The *great light* is truth; truth regarding the negative and destructive thoughts or memories hidden in the darkness of repression. The word *shadow* means *the darkness of error*, sin, resulting in spiritual and physical *death*. *Repent* means *to think differently*, associating it with the *kingdom of heaven*. We enter the kingdom of heaven through a desire to change our life, activating the process that will bring these repressed memories into the light of awareness. Then, at the stage in the process called Naphtali we complete our journey of self-awareness, the holy spirit of our heart revealing the well-hidden emotions that empower the false word of our heart.

When we complete the first ten steps of overcoming a false belief we have judged the negative aspects of the sons of *Leah and the bondmaids,* symbolizing *flesh and bondage.* With each belief we overcome we remove a layer of flesh, coming closer and closer to freedom, like a butterfly emerging from its cocoon. *Twelve* represents *judgment.* Our judgment against the negative aspects of the first *ten* sons of Jacob formulates to *12 x10,* which brings us to the spiritual measure of *120— an hundred and twenty.*

And the Lord said, My Spirit shall not always strive with man, for that he also is flesh: yet his days shall be an hundred and twenty years.

Genesis 6:3

God's holy spirit; the holy spirit of the heart, has exerted much effort in exposing the false perceptions that formed the invisible flesh over our mind, through which we gain an even deeper level of understanding as our holy spirit begins to expose the false beliefs of our heart; exerting much effort in removing the veil of *flesh* over our heart, which is referred to as *"circumcision of the heart"* (Romans 2:29), allowing the seed of truth to enter the heart, as Jesus, the seed or word of God, entered the bowels of the earth following the renting of the veil in the temple.

And Moses was an hundred and twenty years old when he died: his eye was not dim, nor his natural force abated. Deuteronomy 34:7

Moses, symbolizing the *law,* dies when the flesh of our mind dies. We will no longer be in bondage to the fear and lies that once governed out mind, evidence that our mind is now being led by the *holy spirit* of our heart.

But if you are led by the Spirit, you are not under the law.
Galatians 5:18

Moses, symbolizing the *Holy Spirit,* is now more powerful than ever, its *natural force* no longer *abated* by the flesh of the mind. Our holy spirit is now prepared to do its greatest work.

And unto the angel of the church in Sardis write... I know thy works, that thou hast a name that thou livest, and art dead. Be watchful and strengthen [be strong about] *the things which remain, that are ready to die: for I have not found thy works perfect before God. Revelation 3:1,2*

The fifth church of Sardis reveals what we have accomplished through these five days of spiritual works, which formulates to *5 x 24,* which equals *120.* But now we have to be strong when it comes to seeing the things that remain in our heart, which keep us under a spiritual law of bondage. Our mind, immersed in truth, has put our sin in remission. But we must go on to receive the *"gift of the holy spirit"* (Acts 2:38), receiving *truth* in our heart, which the holy spirit of our heart delivers. When the negative and destructive things that remain in the heart are dead, our *works* are completed, made *perfect*.

Sons of the Bondmaids

We are given two orders for the sons born of the bondmaids; the birth order and the last days order. The birth order is Dan and Naphtali, sons of Rachel's bondmaid, followed by Gad and Asher, sons of Leah's bondmaid. Through our judgment (Dan) against the unrighteous word of our heart (Naphtali), we gain power over the destructive spirits that rule through our mind (Gad and Asher). Jesus advocated this method of purification through his cup and platter parable. He taught us that by cleaning the inside of the cup and platter, the outside becomes clean. When the unclean thoughts of our mind and the unclean beliefs of our heart are made pure through truth, there will be no destructive control ruling over our body. Our actions will be pure, in perfect balance. Jesus goes on to explain to us that it is not what is entering in from the outside that defiles us, but what is proceeding out of our heart (Matthew 15:19). Transforming our heart through the light of truth renews our mind, our mind made free of the unholy spirits that once ruled it.

The last days order is Dan, son of Rachel's bondmaid, Gad and Asher, sons of Leah's bondmaid, and Naphtali, son of Rachel's bondmaid. Like the birth order, it starts with judgment (Dan). Only in the last days order the judgment is against the two unholy spirits that work through the mind (Gad and Asher). Due to the addictive state of mankind in the last or end of days, the process must follow this order. Taking action against these two spirits results in a remission; a lessening in the intensity of the destructive energy that is driving the addiction, the body contributing to the power of this remission by lessening the substance or thing that distracts us from, or numbs us to, our feelings. This connection to our emotions will lead us to discovering the false image or belief (Naphtali), all serving to remove the lustful desire we have for whatever it is that for us is dangerous, deadly, or destructive.

Definition of Image

One biblical definition of *image* is *to shade, phantom, i.e. (fig.) illusion, resemblance, a representative figure, esp. an idol-image, vain shew.* Another is *to confine (in the sense of binding); the back of the neck (as that on which burdens are bound).* The image the children of Israel cast in the mount of Sinai symbolizes the image we have formed in our heart. In resisting our holy spirit, as the children of Israel resisted Moses, we reject the divine energy that brings truth; light that transforms our heart, making us free of the false images we have erected there. In rejecting this higher spiritual law the hearts of the children were left unchanged, so their minds could not be trusted to guide their bodies in the right action. Their minds, still in bondage to fear and lies, bound them to a set of laws that forced the mind to control the actions of the body, which the Mosaic Law symbolizes. This physical law, serving to protect them until they learned to obey the spiritual law of the heart, would itself become bondage.

Tell me, ye that desire to be under the law? do ye not hear the law? For it is written that Abraham had two sons, the one by a bondmaid, the other by a freewoman. But he who was of the bondwoman was born after the flesh; but he of the freewoman was by promise. Which things are an allegory: for these are the two covenants; the one from the mount Sinai, which gendereth bondage, which is Hagar. For this Hagar is mount

Sinai in Arabia, and answereth to Jerusalem, which now is, and is in bondage with her children. But Jerusalem which is above is free...
Galatians 4:21-26

Do we want to spend the rest of our life subject to internal and external laws that won't allow us to enjoy the pleasures that were put on this earth for us to enjoy? Do we want to remain bound to a never ending process of recovery? Or bound to a life of hardships because we are too afraid to trust in an internal power that will retrieve us out of bondage, and deliver us into a life of joy and freedom?

Anatomy of an Image
Dissecting the Belief

An image is a god, something we serve. Being a false god, it will have characteristics that mock or imitate the attributes of God the Father. Like a father, who has energy and seed, a god is made up of energy and seed. The Energy or Spirit of God the Father is Love, and His seed or word is truth. The energy or spirit of the other father is fear, and his seed or word is a lie. We have two fathers, with two very different energies, sowing two very different seeds.

Why do ye not understand my speech? even because ye cannot hear my word. Ye are of your father the devil, and the lusts of your father ye will do. He was a murderer from the beginning, and abode not in the truth, because there was no truth in him. When he speaketh a lie, he speaketh of his own: for he is a liar, and the father of it. John 8:43,44

The energy of this *father, the devil* is called *"the energy of delusion,"* the power of the false god, image, or belief. The lie of the mind is the by-product as well as the source of the false belief or image of the heart, the power of which is sustained through painful emotions left unresolved, which leads to hypertension; high blood pressure. The primordial lie, along with its energy of fear, is the first stage in the process that transforms the lie into a false belief, taking it from the mind to the heart. According to the Bible, these lies begin to take hold of the mind of the child just past the age of four, the false belief or image usually cast within the heart of the child by the age of six. To the negative energy of the mind is added the negative energy of the heart, a direct result of the false image that has been erected there. To fear is added anger, which could have been used for the good; to overturn the false images or beliefs of the heart. But we were children, naive and unskilled, the anger remaining, moving into next phase of destructive energy as the spirit of self-will unites with the spirit of anger, resulting in a destructive control; a cruelty unleased upon the body. As long as these false images or other gods remain in that spiritual temple called the heart, so too will their destructive energies of anger and control, which feeds the fear, perpetuating the destructive cycle. We must enter our heart, exposing the false images or beliefs that give power to the fear of our mind, thereby removing the energy or strength of the lie, putting the sin in remission— cancer being the physical manifestation of sin.

If we have an image or belief, religious or personal, that we demonstrate our loyalty to outwardly, we will most likely find ourselves rising up in anger to defend it. We do this out of fear because the belief has been providing us with a false sense of peace and security, of being in control. To give up the image would mean giving up the control. But this is not the type of control we want governing our life; a control whose anger has us hurting ourselves, and others. It can have us numbing ourselves to the pain of our heart instead of connecting with it. It is a control that keeps the emotions that give power to our false beliefs suppressed. We unwittingly seek this control to protect the false image, to keep it alive. This control or will is contrary to the will of love and truth, which is kind and compassionate, the power that should be ruling our thoughts and emotions; a docile will demonstrated through a healthy balanced behavior. No longer will we be driven to care for ourselves through this obstinate will, but through a pure desire that comes out of a Godly love of self.

The dictionary meaning of *image* is *a reproduction of the appearance of someone or something; an object that closely resembles another,* which was formed from what we saw, heard, felt, and experienced throughout our life. And not everything we ate of metaphorically speaking was good. Some of it was evil. But not having the good or right way to compare it to we judged it as good, mistaking evil for good, darkness for light, bitter for sweet, resulting in a life of sorrow instead of one of joy.

To reiterate, an image is a reproduction of the appearance of someone or something. We've discussed the something. Now let's take a look at the someone. How many times in your life have you heard the words, *"you're just like your father"* or *"you're just like your mother"*? The majority of our beliefs come from our father and mother, be they constructive or destructive. The lights of heaven symbolize the perceptions of the mind, coming through the sun and the moon; our father and our mother, and the stars, all of which determine how we think and feel.

The internal component of our image is self-image, and it was our parents or caregivers that were responsible for forming the image we have of our self. They taught us how to feel about our self by how they felt about themselves, reflected in their actions, or in the actions they permitted. If they allowed themselves to be humiliated or intimidated through mental, emotional, sexual, or physical abuse they would have taught us low self-esteem. If they were constantly critical of their own appearance they would have taught us self-loathing. If they suffered with a substance abuse or an eating disorder they would have taught us self-hatred. If they were afraid to step out and take chances to improve the quality of their life they would have taught us self-doubt. We have all eaten of the tree of the knowledge of good and evil. But as we enter into God's spiritual harvest, already in progress, we are to separate the wheat from the chaff; the truth from the lies. Our painful emotions, which hold our false images firmly in place, can never be transformed by a law we institute through our mind, or a discipline we place upon our body. We cannot think or act our way to this deeper level of change. We must feel our way through emotion, looking beyond the bad behavior we saw, which formed an image we may or may not have chosen to reproduce in our life, moving beyond what we thought about these negative behaviors and into how we felt about them. Once we feel the painful emotion we had in connection with a particular experience through the power of our holy spirit, we begin releasing the anger associated with it. The false image or belief, weakened through the release of the anger that sustained it, can now begin the process of being brought down. This begins by validating those painful experiences and the painful emotions associated with them to our self. This level of truth is the light that will enable us to see why we formed these false images or beliefs to begin with. Having the power to scale the wall of our heart, this truth begins to heal the painful emotions that gave power to our false images, levels of light; degrees of truth that make us free of these emotions and beliefs, which have caused us to make some bad decisions throughout our life.

Week 6
Identifying our false images

The knowledge and understanding we gained through the previous weeks of work has given us the ability to identify our false images. This work included acknowledging our repetitive thoughts, and the fear behind them, acknowledging our anger and control, and understanding that we are inhabited with ways of thinking that keep us stuck in patterns, repeating the same mistakes over and over again, going around and around in circles, stuck in the same miserable place, bound to the same unsatisfying life, or to the same destructive habits. This cyclic nature was illustrated by the children of Israel when they formed and worshipped the calf or *heifer*, meaning *circular, to revolve*. They sacrificed the red heifer in the wilderness, symbolizing the sacrificing of this dangerous cyclic nature of ours. Whatever takes up most of our mental energy, whatever we strive most to obtain, try hardest to control, or rise up in anger to defend, is pointing to the false belief that has us going around and around in circles, making no spiritual advancement.

We judge Naphtali by understanding that the words we spoke in our heart through painful emotions formed false images or beliefs that cannot be overcome by just thinking positive thoughts. The color associated with Naphtali is violet.

Chapter Eleven
Judging Joseph

Joseph is a fruitful bough, even a fruitful bough by a well; whose branches run over the wall. The archers have sorely grieved him, and shot at him, and hated him: But his bow abode in strength, and the arms of his hands were made strong by the hands of the mighty God of Jacob (from thence is the shepherd, the stone of Israel;) Even by the God of thy father, who shall help thee; and by the Almighty, who shall bless thee with blessings of heaven above, blessings of the deep that lieth under, blessings of the breasts and of the womb: The blessings of thy father have prevailed above the blessings of my progenitors unto the utmost bound of the everlasting hills: they shall be on the head of Joseph, and on the crown of the head of him that was separate from his brethren.

Genesis 49:22-26

J oseph is the first son born of Rachel, the one Jacob loved. *Rachel* symbolizes the *Heart*, and *Joseph* symbolizes the *first fruit of the Heart.* The word *Joseph* means *let him add,* and what is to be added to the heart is truth. Some truths come through the power of the mind; through study, analysis, or deductive reasoning. But the deeper truths come through the power of the heart; through intuition and revelation. The word *bough* means *to build; a son (builder of the family name).* When the word of truth is conceived in our heart it builds upon the family name because the family name *is* truth. Through the conception of truth within our heart we become *a son,* which is pleasing to God.

even a fruitful bough by a well; ...

The *bough* symbolizes the *heart*. The *well* symbolizes the *deep understanding* that comes to our mind through the *branches* of the bough; through the *anointing of spirit* and *truth*.

What be these two branches which through the two golden pipes empty the golden oil out of themselves? ... Knowest thou not what these be? And I said, No, my lord. Then said he, These are the two anointed ones, that stand by the Lord of the whole earth.   Zechariah 4:12-14

whose branches run over the wall ...

The *branches run over the wall* when the holy spirit moves the truth over the wall of flesh that covers the heart. Spirit and truth; the golden healing anointing that passes through the mind and heart, symbolized by the *two golden pipes*.

The archers have sorely grieved him, and shot at him, and hated him: ...

The *archers* symbolize the *adversaries of truth*. We have become these spiritual archers, having grieved the truth of our own heart through every belief that we accepted into our heart that was not true.

But his bow abode in strength, and the arms of his hands were made strong by the hands of the mighty God of Jacob...

The *bow* of Joseph is the *power* behind the truth, which is our holy spirit. It shoots *arrows* in the good sense; shooting *words of truth* into our mind and heart. This is a very subtle and spontaneous action, evoked through the quieting of the mind. The evidence that it is taking place will be in the new and positive way we are beginning to feel as we go through this process of being delivered of our false beliefs.

And Elisha said unto him, Take bow and arrows. And he took unto him bow and arrows. And he said to the king of Israel, put thine hand upon the bow, And he put his hand upon it: and Elisha put his hands upon the king's hands. And he said, Open the window eastward. And he opened it. Then Elisha said, Shoot. And he shot. And he said, The arrow of the Lord's deliverance... 2 Kings 13:15-17

Elisha symbolizes the spiritual power that delivers us from bondage through the resurrection of truth (2 Kings 13:21).

Even by the God of thy father, who shall help thee; and by the Almighty, who shall bless thee with blessings of heaven above, blessings of the deep that lieth under, blessings of the breasts and of the womb: ...

God helps us through His two anointed ones; through His spirit and word. And we, being made in the image of God, have access to it. God helps us when we call upon this spiritual power to help ourselves. The *blessings of heaven* and the *blessings of the deep* is the good that comes from having the thoughts and emotions that are buried deep within us brought up to the surface; into our awareness. Through this awareness we receive the *blessings of the breasts and of the womb;* the gracious gift of nurturing ourselves through the truth that we have conceived of within that spiritual womb called the heart. If truth rules our heart, love will rule our mind, the fear of our mind and the falsehood of our heart abolished for good. This state is being referred to as *"Christ consciousness."* The New Testament refers to is as having *"the mind of Christ"* (1 Corinthians 2:16). The word *Christ* means *anointed,* the anointing of spirit and truth; the *"two olive trees or branches"* that empty out their golden oil through the *two golden pipes,* symbolizing our *mind and heart.*

The blessings of thy father have prevailed above the blessings of my progenitors unto the utmost bound of the everlasting hills: ...

(King James Bible)

May the blessings of your father transcend the blessings of the mountains eternal, the bounds of hills without age. (The Five Books of Moses)

115

The *blessings* that come through spirit and truth transcend the physical, reaching into the spiritual to heal the soul.

they shall be on the head of Joseph, and on the crown of the head of him that was separate from his brethren.

The *head of Joseph* is the *authority of truth,* which carries the blessings of heaven and earth through the creation of a new heaven and earth; a new mind and heart, through which we enter a new state of being. Joseph was separated from his brothers when they threw him in a pit, illustrating how the negative forces of our mind work together to destroy the truth of our heart. The *crown of the head* reveals the *humbled posture* of this process, through which we completely separate ourselves from these destructive forces of the mind, receiving a spiritual crown, symbolizing the rule we have over them (Revelation 2:26, 27).

After Joseph separates from his brothers, he finds himself in Egypt, in the World, but not of the world; no longer influenced by the principalities of darkness that once ruled the mind. Soon after entering Egypt Joseph is falsely accused by a woman and thrown into prison. We are not free yet! The *woman* symbolizes the *flesh* formed by our word of error, which keeps us in bondage. There is more work to do!

While in the solitude of prison, Joseph comes in contact with the *baker* and the *butler,* symbolizing the *spirit* and *word* of God, which we connect with when we are still. Each man has a dream, which Joseph interprets. The chief butler's dream reveals the reinstating of his butlership, but the baker's dream reveals the lifting off of his head, history repeating itself two thousand years later when the head of John the Baptist was lifted off, while Jesus went on to teach the gospel of truth. John preached *repentance,* meaning *to think differently.* But it was time to put an end to the *dead works* of repentance, and go on into perfection. John instructs his disciples to stop following him and follow Jesus, who was teaching perfection through the purification of the heart.

Through the eastern practice of quieting the mind, the holy spirit of our heart is put in a position of authority, which it uses to influence our mind, causing us to repent or think differently, changing our mind. This is the work of the *spirit* of God. When we are forced by the onset of disease to care for ourselves, an act of loving ourselves, we are combining the *spirit* of love with the *word* of truth, the latter applied through the wisdom of traditional and alternative medicine, through which the body receives her healing. But to heal the soul, which is perfection, we must be healed of our painful emotions through the transformation of our heart. This is the work of the *word* of God. This resurrection of truth within the heart changes the way we feel, the spirit of love reaching its highest degree through the word of truth.

And Pharaoh said unto his servants, Can we find such a one as this is, a man in whom the Spirit of God is. And Pharaoh said unto Joseph, Forasmuch as God hath shewed thee all this, there is none so discreet and wise as thou art: Genesis 41:38,39

It was the *Spirit of truth,* the culmination of spirit and truth that gave Joseph the ability to interpret dreams, and to predict the future.

Howbeit when he, the Spirit of truth is come, he will lead you into all truth...for he shall not speak of himself; but whatsoever he shall hear, that shall he speak: and he will shew you things to come. John 16:13

Joseph became a high priest *"after the order of Melchisedec"* (Psalms 110:4; Hebrews 6:20). He followed a specific order, making sacrifice for himself first, getting his own life in order. This put him in a position of authority, which he used to sacrifice for the people, expending time and effort to help others.

Interpreting Dreams

And Pharaoh said unto Joseph, I have dreamed a dream, and there is none that can interpret it: and I have heard said of thee, that thou canst understand a dream to interpret it. Genesis 41:15

Dreams come from the heart or subconscious. If we are wise, we will internalize these dreams until we complete our transformation process. Our dreams, more often than not, are revealing what is taking place within us spiritually; mentally and emotionally. They are spiritual messengers, serving to bring us a greater understanding of ourselves, showing us areas we need to work on so we can reach perfection. Those having reached a degree of spiritual maturity will perceive their dreams as such, but the spiritual child, needing constant assurance that everything he is doing is right, will not. But if we want to become spiritual adults, our soul reaching full maturity, we will have to grow up, overcoming the fear of coming face to face with ourselves.

For we know in part, and we prophecy in part. But when that which is perfect is come, then that which is in part shall be done away with. When I was a child, I spake as a child, I thought as a child: but when I became a man, I put away childish things. For now we see through a glass darkly; but then face to face; now I know in part; but then shall I know even as I am known. 1 Corinthians 13:9-12

Joseph, like Jesus, symbolizes truth, and we must receive truth from within in order to receive pure truth pertaining to things without. The Spirit of truth will bring us truth, but if our motivation is not pure; if we are not seeking truth to purify our mind and heart first, then the truth pertaining to things physical will be passing through a filter, distorting the truth. This is why it is so important to sacrifice all, offering up everything we think we know to be true. If we put it all on the altar, that which remains, after the false images are consumed, will be pure truth. In this is our protection!

Joseph came face to face with himself during his time in prison. In communing with the baker and the butler, the spirit and the word or the *christ,* Joseph would have come into a great deal of truth about himself, as the woman at the well received a deep understanding of her life through Jesus, of whom she spoke, saying, *"Come, see a man, which told me all things that I ever did: is not this the Christ?* (John 4:29). He didn't reveal prophecies, or speak of a kingdom in a faraway place. He gave her something to drink; something to think about with regard to her own life, causing her to question the circumstances of her life. What belief caused her to repeat the same mistake over and over again? What image had her attracting men incapable of committing to a relationship? She sought to answer these questions in the stillness of her mind, as Joseph sought to answer questions pertaining to his own life in the solitude of prison.

When we quiet our mind, our holy spirit is able to influence our mind, persuading us to ask the right questions, the answers coming through the power of our holy spirit, which brings the light of truth that enables us to transform our life. Joseph was probably around eighteen when he entered prison. By age thirty his word was authority, ruling all of Egypt. Twelve years, in which he completed his own spiritual judgment or transformation process, yet another parallel between Joseph and Jesus. They made sacrifice for themselves first by going through the healing process, which was the duty of the high priest. He makes sacrifice for himself first, then for the people. Joseph and Jesus both went on to make sacrifice for the people. Joseph by gathering the literal corn that fed them in the physical famine, and Jesus by gathering the spiritual corn of spiritual truth, which will feed the people during the spiritual famine (Amos 8:11).

And Joseph was thirty years old when he stood before Pharaoh king of Egypt. And Joseph went out from the presence of Pharaoh, and went throughout all the land of Egypt. Genesis 41:46

Under Jewish law, the age at which a man can qualify to become a high priest is thirty, which is believed to be the age of Jesus when he began to go throughout the land teaching the spiritual word of God, feeding them with spiritual corn. When our heart conceives of God's word of truth through the completion of our six metaphorical days of spiritual works, our new spiritual heaven and earth is finished, as God's creation of heaven and earth, made through the works that is His word, was finished in whatever period of time constitutes six days with God. The sixth day of work correlates with the sixth church of Philadelphia:

And unto the angel of the church in Philadelphia write; These things saith he that is holy, he that is true, HE THAT HATH THE KEY OF DAVID, HE THAT OPENETH, AND NO MAN SHUTTETH; AND SHUTTETH, AND NO MAN OPENETH; I know thy works: behold, I have set before thee an open door, and no man can shut it: for thou hast a little strength, and hast kept my word, and hast not denied my name... hold fast which thou hast, that no man take thy crown. Him that overcometh will I make a pillar in the temple of my God, and he shall go no more out: and I will write upon him the name of my God, and the name of the city of my God, which is new Jerusalem, which cometh down out of heaven from my God: and I will write upon him my new name. Revelation 3:7-12

We are made *holy* through the spirit and *true* through the word. We receive the word by doing the works; overcoming every false belief accepted in our heart throughout our life. *THE KEY OF DAVID* is *LOVE,* the Spirit that brings the light that exposes our false word of false beliefs. In sacrificing our word of error we resurrect the word of truth, ruling ourselves in righteousness, through which we will do the

120

right thing, choosing the right action. Standing as *a pillar* of righteousness we are now qualified to support others as they go through the process of opening up their hearts to truth, helping guide them in a positive direction in their life.

And Jesus said unto them, Verily I say unto you, That ye which have followed me, in the regeneration when the Son of man shall sit in the throne of his glory, ye also shall sit upon twelve thrones, judging the twelve tribes of Israel. Matthew 19:28

The word *regeneration* means *the act or process of creating anew*, referring to the creation of our new spiritual heaven and earth— *new Jerusalem*. The number *twelve* represents *judgment*. Our judgment against the negative aspects of the twelve tribes of Israel formulates to *12x12*, bringing us to the spiritual measure of *144— an hundred and forty and four.*

And he measured the wall thereof, an hundred and forty and four cubits, according to the measure of a man... Revelation 21:17

Through the completion of these internal works we measure up to God's standard. Having built up the walls of the new Jerusalem through God's spirit of love and word of truth we enter an invisible wall of protection (Psalms 51:18). As a new mother, which new Jerusalem symbolizes, we will protect through positive emotions the good seed or word of truth we have conceived of within our heart.

And I saw a new heaven and a new earth: for the first heaven and the first earth were passed away; and there was no more sea... And God shall wipe away all tears from their eyes; and there shall be no more death, neither sorrow, nor crying, neither shall there be any more pain: for the former things are passed away... Behold, I make all things new.
Revelation 21:1,4

Our *first heaven and earth* passes away through the creation of *a new heaven and earth,* symbolizing *a new mind and heart.* There is no more *sea* because the *thoughts hidden in the depths* of our mind have been brought to light, exposing the painful emotions that lie beneath them, which have likewise been transformed through the light of truth. The love we have for ourselves, which we first start to demonstrate by not resisting the power that brings us truth, will begin to flow out to our brothers, which is the message of the sixth church of Asia, *Philadelphia,* meaning, *brotherly love.* *"Love thy neighbor as thyself."* It starts with the self.

Summary

The untruthful thoughts we took into our mind became the untruthful beliefs we conceived of within our heart, bringing us into spiritual darkness, causing us to make some bad decisions in our life. To bring ourselves back into the light will require us to activate the spiritual energy that brings us into light, which has been bound by the source of power that resists it— the mind. Shutting off the everyday thoughts of our mind gives a voice to the holy spirit of our heart, which speaks to us through the memories that have been hidden in the depths of our subconscious, moving them up into our awareness. The repression of these painful memories formed a mental wall, behind which our painful emotions hide. It is our awareness of these hidden thoughts or memories called *"the lower waters"* or *"sea"* that allows us to see what lies beneath them in our heart. With the door of our heart open we become aware of the emotions we have suppressed. Once we connect with these emotions we will no longer be able to hold on to the false peace that kept our mind from connecting with our heart. Now the process that removes our word of error, the false beliefs that formed the flesh that covers our heart, can begin, which is *"circumcision of the heart"*

(Romans 2:29). Through the power of truth, every false image or belief that has been set up on *"the fleshy tables of the heart"* will be overturned, removing a layer of flesh with each false image or belief we judge or overcome.

The negative and destructive emotional energy associated with the painful things from our past, along with the lie we told ourselves in those times, formed our false beliefs, giving them the power to run our lives in a negative and destructive way. Releasing these emotions through the mind and body disciplines described in this book shakes the foundation upon which these false images or beliefs were built. The truth or self-validation of the painful things that took place, along with the truth of how we felt about them, strikes another blow to the false image or belief. Truth is the spiritual light that transforms our negative and destructive energy into positive and constructive or creative energy. With the heart void of the evil seeds of false beliefs, it is able to conceive of the good seed or word of truth.

Week 7
Sowing the word of truth

This is the third and final phase of the process, which like the first phase, is accomplished through the power of the mind, which is now being influenced by our holy spirit. Through the previous weeks of work we will have transformed the negative energy in our thoughts and emotions by bringing them out of darkness and into the light, bringing down the wall of flesh formed by our lies and false beliefs. Now when we speak a positive word it will not hit the wall. It will penetrate the heart, the good seed conceived through the power of positive emotion. Whatever negative self-image we had about ourselves can now be replaced with a new positive self-image. Maybe we held the belief that we were stupid.

Well now when we tell ourselves we are not stupid, our self will believe it, our heart able to accept this seed of truth, which will not get choked out by lies this time around. And what we believe in our heart we will live, demonstrated through a new found trust and confidence in ourselves as we make right decisions from a pure heart. Our thoughts will be right thoughts, our motivations pure, driven by the pure spirit and pure truth now residing in our heart. The consequences of our actions will be constructive rather than destructive. We will experience success rather than failure, joy rather than sorrow. We will have rewritten our book of life by replacing the false word inscribed upon the tablets of our heart with the word of truth.

We judge Joseph by completing the process, overcoming our word of error through the word of truth. The color associated with Joseph is white, the result of combining all seven colors, symbolized by Joseph's coat of many colors.

Chapter Twelve
Judging Benjamin

Benjamin shall ravin as a wolf: in the morning he shall devour the prey, and at night he shall divide the spoil. Genesis 49:27

B enjamin was the second son born of Rachel, the one Jacob loved. *Rachel* symbolizes the *Heart*, and *Benjamin* the *second fruit of the Heart*. Benjamin, like Reuben, symbolizes the spirit, be it holy or unholy. The word *ravin* means *to pluck off or pull to pieces, to supply with food*. The word *wolf* means *to be yellow*, which is slang for the word coward; one who lacks courage in the face of danger or pain. The negative aspect of Reuben is fear, the opposite of courage, and which opposes love. This is the unholy spirit we battle as we go through this process that begins with Reuben and ends with Benjamin. The negative aspect of Benjamin is the false belief, one that many are feeding on out of fear, and impatience. It is a popular belief because it offers an easy solution, allowing one, through the deception of his mind, to arrive at the destination without taking the journey, which is to go within and discover the danger of ones hidden thoughts and the pain of ones hidden emotions. The unholy spirit of Benjamin or the false belief is fear, the negative energy that has many skipping over the pain of the heart through denial, delusion, drugs, religion, etc., skipping over the emotional pain inherent in the spiritual birthing process; an essential constituent or characteristic of the birthing process!

Before she travailed, she brought forth, before her pain came, she was delivered of a man child. Who hath heard such a thing? Who hath seen such things? Shall the earth be made to bring forth in one day? Or shall a nation be born at once? Isaiah 66:7,8

The word *Reuben* means *see ye a son.* A *son* symbolizes *full maturity, a perfected state,* which is accomplished by completing the process revealed through the twelve sons of Jacob. The birth cannot be forced. It takes time, and involves pain and hard labor. It takes work! We cannot think our way, control our way, or pray our way to this birth. We cannot call upon God to change us. We must change ourselves by calling upon the divine attributes of God. Proclaiming we have given birth before we have gone through the pain of labor will result in an *"untimely birth,"* the soul never reaching full maturity. Believing we have reached an ascended state before we have completed the spiritual works or labor that equates to spiritual ascension is the *deception of iniquity.*

... and with every deception of iniquity to those that are perishing, because they admitted not the love of the truth in order that they might be saved. And on this account God will send to them the energy of delusion, to their believing the falsehood. 2 Thessalonians 2:10,11 (Greek Diaglott)

Our *love of the truth* activates the anointing, *christ,* without which there can be no salvation. And what we are saved from is our self; from the destructive beliefs that inhabit our heart, which speak through the negative and destructive thoughts of our conscious and subconscious mind. What spirit is leading us? Does it have us seeking mind peace over heart peace? Experiencing outer dimensions instead of inner ones? Does it have us entering into states of consciousness for any other purpose than to enter into our own heart? God's holy spirit will lead us into that spiritual temple called the heart, where we will sacrifice our false images, thereby giving life to the *word of truth;* to the *son,* to Benjamin in the positive sense, the

126

word *Benjamin* meaning *son of the right hand,* the right hand symbolizing power— *son of the power of God.*

Reuben, thou art my firstborn, my might, and the beginning of my strength, the excellency of dignity, and the excellency of power.

Genesis 49:3

Through this process we come full circle, revitalizing the spirit of love through the word of truth, bringing it back to the state in which we received it from God— perfect.

And they journeyed from Bethel; and there was but a little way to come to Ephrath: and Rachel travailed, and she had hard labor. And it came to app, when she was in hard labor, that the midwife said unto her, Fear not; thou shalt have this son also. And it came to pass, as her soul was in departing, (for she died) that she called his name Benoni: but his father called him Benjamin. Genesis 35:16-18

Rachel symbolizes the Heart, which brings forth Joseph and Benjamin. If we give birth to Joseph, giving birth to truth from within our heart, we will also give birth to Benjamin, love, which is the spirit of truth, as fear is the spirit of a lie. The word *Benoni* means *son of my sorrow,* the result of not giving birth to truth from within our heart.

A Misconception of Love

From the beginning we formed the wrong concept of love. We were taught that love equates to having external power. We cried, and our external world reacted, which formed this image that love is something expressed toward us through some external act. We have come to equate love with a physical act. Mankind has been externalizing the spirit attribute of God, demonstrating love through external acts of kindness, which while making us feel good, does not have the power to heal our soul. That will require the holy spirit to transcend the boundaries of the physical through an internal act. If we continue to only express our love through physical acts, we will never heal our world of its many problems, the roots of which are spiritual. We must direct this love toward our self. Allowing the holy spirit of our heart to bring us the truth that transforms the negative and destructive energy bottled up in us into positive energy, is a deeper act of love.

Thou shalt love thy neighbor as thyself. James 2:8.

The power to love our neighbor comes out of the power to love our self. We cannot heal our world with love until we heal our hearts with truth. Only then will our love have the power of truth, the power needed to transform our world.

And he shewed me a pure river of water of life, clear as crystal, proceeding out of the throne of God and of the Lamb. In the midst of the street of it, and on either side of the river, was there the tree of life, which bare twelve manner of fruits, and yielded her fruit every month: and the leaves were for the healing of the nations. Revelation 22:1,2

We are *the tree of life,* bearing *twelve manner of fruits* in the good sense by judging, overcoming, the negative aspects of the twelve sons of Jacob or twelve tribes of Israel. This process, God's 12-step healing process, is *the healing of the nations;* spiritual nations that exist in our own mind and heart, which we are given power over through the completion of our six metaphorical days of spiritual works. (Revelation 2:26).

And Jesus said unto them, Verily I say unto you, That ye which have followed me, in the regeneration when the Son of man shall sit in the throne of his glory, ye also shall sit upon twelve thrones, judging the twelve tribes of Israel. Matthew 19:28

The word *regeneration* means *the act or process of creating anew,* referring to the creation of a new heaven and earth, symbolizing a new mind and heart.

God's counsel to those skipping over the spiritual works:

And unto the angel of the church of Laodiceans write; These things saith the Amen, the faithful and true witness, the beginning of the creation of God; ... Because thou sayest, I am rich, and increased with goods, and have need of nothing; and knowest not that thou art wretched, and miserable, and poor, and blind, and naked: I counsel thee to buy of me gold tried in the fire, that thou mayest be rich; and white raiment, that thou mayest be clothed, and that the shame of thy nakedness do not appear; and anoint thine eyes with eyesalve, that thou mayest see.

Revelation 3:14-18

These are at the *beginning of the creation* process, having six days of works to perform, through which they would form a new spiritual heaven and earth. What you think you are in the delusion of your mind is not what you are in the reality of your heart, a connection that can only be made by getting in touch with the hidden thoughts of your mind and the hidden emotions of your heart. The *gold tried in the fire* symbolizes *the internal judgment* through which the impurities of the heart (Matthew 15:19) are removed, leaving only *gold,* symbolizing *purity.* Through this judgment we become spiritually *rich;* rich in spirit and in truth. The *white raiment* symbolizes the spiritual *wedding garment,* the evidence that one has been compliant with God's salvation or purification process. The *eyesalve* is *truth,* giving us the ability to see our life, which is transformed by following the instruction provided through God's ancient 12-step healing process. Upon completion of this process we will have a new heart, the feelings of which will have changed the dynamics of our relationships. Those that were an extension of our old energy will end, while new ones, an extension of our new energy, begin. We will stand for what is right, living the new truth of our heart, which being the precious seed of God, we will protect with a wall of positive emotions, protecting our heart, separating ourselves from those that are emotionally toxic. This is a demonstration of love; not only for our self, but for those we separated from, having helped enable their bad behavior. Putting the burden back on them we compel them to carry their own cross, putting them in a position that we can only hope will have them crying out, activating the process through which they too will be healed. Those that are experiencing this life-changing process will surely recognize it in the words of this little book for the soul.

We judge Benjamin by overcoming the fear of leaving behind any belief that stands in the way of our salvation, the outcome of this extraordinary healing process. The color associated with Benjamin is red, the color of spirit. The color of truth is white. Together they make pink; the highest degree, the finest example— the color of complete healing.

Jacob's ladder

And he dreamed, and behold a ladder set up on the earth, and the top of it reached to heaven: and behold the angels of God ascending and descending on it. Genesis 28:12

The *ladder* symbolizes the *process of transformation,* which is set up on the *earth,* symbolizing the *heart.* The *angels* are *spiritual messengers,* which ascend and descend, bringing messages from the heart to the mind and back again. The steps of the ladder are taken simultaneously as we apply the message of each son to overcome each false belief of our heart. With each false belief we remove we peel away a layer of flesh, along with its negative and destructive energy, removing more and more density, ascending through degrees of spiritual or vibrational energy until we reach the highest realm of our spiritual potential, which is to be mentally, emotionally, and physically free, which *is* salvation of the soul!

So Relax, and take a deep breath as you begin your journey of internal transformation. It is an au natural birthing process that ultimately takes place through the spontaneous feelings of the heart, not through the self-willed thoughts of the mind. Enjoy the experience, and work with the contractions that come through the painful emotions that will deliver you into the new person you are about to become. This is the most important work you will ever do. Through this amazing healing process we return to that spiritual state we once knew as children. When our mind, heart, and body were pure, and our soul was free.

Godspeed

Introduction to Astrology *by Jeffrey Brock*

Because of the prevalent misconceptions regarding Astrology, and what can be done with it, the following points can be studied to the advantage of the student. Astrology has nothing to do with either fortune telling or fatalism. The former is superstition, pretending to the impossible, such as the exact prediction of exact events on definite dates, which is impossible at our present state of knowledge. The latter is simply a form of escapism, an effort to avoid responsibility for our actions.

Serious Astrology is the practical application of two very ancient doctrines. The first is generally formulated in the phrase "As Above, So Below;" the second has come to be termed by Carl Jung a "synchronism." Implicit in the first of these ideas is that the Universe is a unity in itself and so if we can measure one part of it, from that we can deduce another part. So, as we can measure the pattern of the heavens as formed in space and time, from that patterning we can deduce the pattern of our lives as they are lived in space and time. "As Above, So Below." Implicit in the second concept that anything that happens in any given moment of time contains within itself the qualities and potentialities of that moment. All future development, for good or for ill, depends upon the initiatory impulse and the use made of it. As Carl Jung said, " We are born at a given moment, in a given place, like vintage years of wine, we have the qualities of the year and the season in which we are born. Astrology does not lay claim to anything more." Astrology is therefore the science of correspondences and the study of beginnings.

Astrology is primarily a guide to self-knowledge, the first requisite for the achievement of happiness and success in life. The chart shows the pattern of our lives, the general trends and the influences operative, the choices we shall have to make and how we can work out our lives to the greater advantage. In a very real sense character is destiny, and what happens to us is the result, direct or indirect, of our own actions, our own characters, what we have been, or done, at some time in our evolution up to the present period. Everything that comes to us is our own, and what we do now determines what will come to us in the achievement of successful development in those things which, in the last analysis are of primary importance. The material indications furnished by the chart are of secondary importance. Apparent good fortune on the material planes, coming to one who has not the mental and spiritual ability to enjoy it, is like giving a library to a man who cannot read.

It is to be understood that this ancient science/art furnishes us with an ability to comprehend causations and a knowledge of cycles that stems from Cosmic Law.

Biography of *Jeffrey Brock*

Jeffrey Brock, C.A.P., C.ht. is the owner/director of the Astrological & Metaphysical Research Center in Miami, Florida. He has been practicing astrology professionally since 1976 and has been teaching in the field since 1978. Jeffrey has been a frequent speaker with the NCGR – Florida Atlantic Chapter and the S.F.A.A - South Florida Astrological Association on the subject of Medical Astrology. His expertise in the area of health and healing stems from an extensive background in the natural foods industry. He is also a wonderful "star-gazing" guide and has lead groups on field trips to observe the constellations first-hand.

(The contents of this book do not necessarily reflect the views of Jeffrey Brock).

Book References

The Authorized King James Version of the Bible

The Five Books of Moses   The Schocken Bible   Volume 1

The Emphatic Diaglott

The New Strong's Exhaustive Concordance of the
Bible *by James Strong,* LL.D, S.T.D.

Heal Your Body *by Louise L. Hay*

The American Heritage Dictionary

Index to Scripture References

Index to Scripture References

Index to Scripture References

Index to Scripture References

Notes

Notes

Notes

Notes

Notes

Notes

Notes

Notes

Notes

Notes

Notes

Notes